Discourses of Legitimation in the News

Examining the news coverage of the economic crisis in Greece, this book develops a framework for identifying discourses of legitimation of actors, political decisions, and policies in the news.

This study departs from the assumption that news is a privileged terrain where discursive struggles (over power) are represented and take place. Incorporating systematic analysis of news texts and journalistic practices, the model contextualises the analysis in its specific socio-political environment and examines legitimising discourse through the prism of the news. Ultimately the book recognises the active role played by journalists and media in legitimating economic crisis related policies and decisions, and how they help dominant actors establish and legitimate their authority, which in turn helps journalists legitimate their own role and authority.

A concise, focussed book that applies a strong theoretical and methodological framework, *Discourses of Legitimation in the News* is a strong contribution to the field for researchers and postgraduate students.

Vaia Doudaki works as a senior researcher at Charles University in Prague. In the past, she worked as an associate professor at Uppsala University, and as a lecturer and assistant professor at the Cyprus University of Technology. Her research is situated in the fields of alternative media studies, journalism studies, and discourse studies. Her latest book (co-edited with Nico Carpentier) is *Cyprus and its conflicts. Representations, materialities and cultures* (2018).

Angeliki Boubouka is a professional journalist and an independent media researcher. She has been practicing journalism for print and online media in Greece, since 1993. She has also worked as a research associate for the Department of Communication and Internet Studies at Cyprus University of Technology. Her work on the news framing of the economic crisis in Greece and in Cyprus has been published in *Journalism* and in *European Journal of Communication.*

Discourses of Legitimation in the News

The Case of the Economic Crisis in Greece

Vaia Doudaki and Angeliki Boubouka

Routledge
Taylor & Francis Group
LONDON AND NEW YORK

First published 2020
by Routledge
2 Park Square, Milton Park, Abingdon, Oxon OX14 4RN

and by Routledge
52 Vanderbilt Avenue, New York, NY 10017

Routledge is an imprint of the Taylor & Francis Group, an informa business

British Library Cataloguing-in-Publication Data
A catalogue record for this book is available from the British Library

Library of Congress Cataloging-in-Publication Data
A catalog record for this book has been requested

ISBN: 978-0-367-18394-3 (hbk)
ISBN: 978-0-429-06132-5 (ebk)

Typeset in Times New Roman
by Apex CoVantage, LLC

Contents

Figures and tables

Figures

Tables

Introduction

Assumptions and foundations

Vaia Doudaki

This study departs from the assumption that news is a privileged terrain where discursive struggles (over power) are represented and take place. Using as a case study the news coverage of the economic crisis in Greece, this book explores the discourses of legitimation of political decisions, actors, and policies in the news. Legitimation in this study relates to the establishment of a sense of beneficial, ethical, or necessary action in specific settings (Vaara 2014, 503; Vaara and Tienari 2008, 986). The analysis of news related to the economic crisis aims at the identification of the struggles over legitimation and authority building of the protagonists of the economic crisis in Greece. In this book, we study how these leading actors attempt to establish a consensual perception of legitimacy to their actions and authority and discredit those of their opponents, creating "realities that advance their interests", in their effort "to achieve discursive dominance" (Reshef and Keim 2014, 18).

The research focusses specifically on the periods and events related to the signing of the three Memoranda (bailout agreements) in 2010, 2011–2012, and 2015, between Greece and the Troika (i.e. the European Union [EU], the European Central Bank [ECB], and the International Monetary Fund [IMF]), which were presented as "necessary for the salvation" of the Greek economy, and the period around the completion of the terms of the third Memorandum (in 2018), which is seen as indicating the stabilisation of Greece's economy. Throughout the analysis of news articles from two Greek leading newspapers – *Ta Nea* and *I Kathimerini* – it is demonstrated how the elite news sources that appear in the domestic mainstream press attempt to legitimate or delegitimate policies and measures related to the bailout agreements and their implications. In addition, it is demonstrated how, through their privileged presence in the news, these elite sources are given ample opportunities to legitimate their own positions and establish their authority.

As it happens in any research endeavour, also this one is informed by a set of epistemological (and ideological, as no scientific enterprise is ideology-free) assumptions. The first one concerns the economic crisis. For the purposes of this research, a crisis is seen as "a (highly) disruptive event or situation leading to disorder or even disaster, significantly disturbing the lives of people or the relations among individuals and groups" (Doudaki and Carpentier 2018, 2; see also Vecchi 2009; Coombs 2015, 3–4). This study thus assumes that a predicament exists in Greece that bears significant implications for the lives of many people. Also, there is the assumption or the expectation, embedded in the use of the term "economic crisis", that there is a specific starting point and, more importantly, an end point to the crisis. Still, as this study argues, the components, dimensions, and time span of this disruptive situation labelled as crisis, are not clear-cut; they are rather politically, economically, and culturally articulated, interpreted, negotiated, contested, and reinterpreted. Within this logic, the answers to what the constituents of the crisis are, when a crisis starts and when it ends, who is affected and how, who is responsible, and who can provide solutions, are contingent, time- and context-sensitive, and the (temporary) outcome of interactions and power dynamics (see, e.g. Doudaki et al. 2016, 2019).

Furthermore, one dimension not specifically addressed in this study, which still needs to be taken in consideration, is the construction of the economy and the economic system: as the "crisis" is defined through the malfunctioning of basic components and features of the economic system, the economic system itself is largely constructed via the articulation of performance standards, perils, tools for recovery, etc., through a discursive struggle around what constitutes a crisis (which in turn is depended on who is affected and, most importantly, on who participates in the discursive struggle).

In times of economic turmoil, the material conditions for large groups of people change significantly, affecting their lives at multiple levels. Relatedly, economic policies implemented to deal with the turmoil have repercussions that are directly visible, on people and societies, more so than, for example, the state policies on culture and education. Furthermore, during these times, severe socio-political conflicts arise, "regarding the (re)distribution of resources and the struggle over the endorsed models of social, political and economic organization" (Doudaki and Carpentier 2018, 9). These tensions have a disruptive potential on the established power relations among the different socio-political groups, creating "opportunities for rearticulation of the main discourses about the organisation of the state and its institutions" (ibid., 14).

All these phenomena are (re)presented and (re)constructed in and through the news, to a large extent. As Gaye Tuchman argues, "news does not mirror society. It helps to constitute it as a shared social phenomenon, for in the process of describing an event, news defines and shapes that event" (1978, 184).

> In fact, far from offering neutral accounts of events, news acts rather as a carrier of dense cultural and ideological symbols reflecting popular beliefs and the power dynamics of societies, being one of the main sources of knowledge and power in society (Entman 2004; Tuchman 1978, 217).
>
> (Doudaki 2018, 143)

Within this logic, news media and journalists play a crucial role in constructing the phenomenon of the economic crisis, and mediating the public debate over the issue and its dimensions, thus providing the space not only for power struggles, but also for the (de)legitimation of actors, policies, and authorities.

Equally important in the construction of the crisis phenomenon in the news, and the articulation of certain types of discourses around it, is the role of news sources. Being the product of a series of decisions of inclusion, exclusion, and priming, by journalists and news media (see, e.g. Hall et al. 1978; Gitlin 1980), the presence of sources in the news is highly instrumental, leading to the dominance of specific types of actors, representing mainly the political, economic, and other institutional elites (Reese 1990; Gitlin 1980). The reasons for privileging these kinds of sources are related to the journalists' perceptions of professional practice; the media's affiliation to specific economic and political interests; and the co-orientation of the main societal institutions and their actors (news media and journalists being among them) towards the same values regarding the organisation of society, sharing, in a symbiotic relationship, the same vision for the world.

Through their privileged presence in the news, institutional news sources are given the opportunity to not only present the pieces of information and facts that support their positions (while omitting others that might be unfavourable or damaging for them), but also to claim and (re)legitimate their authority, and delegitimise the authority position of other actors. The instrumental use of news sources is of particular importance also for the validation of the dominant model of objective journalism, as it reflects the convention of the detached, neutral reporting of events based on data collected through the journalists' sources (Berkowitz 2009). The objectivity norm serves the establishment of journalistic authority also in relation to how news is constructed into an identifiable cultural product. As it is argued in this study, news is a product of the inherent tension stemming from its dual factual/

narrative nature, and a lot of the conventions in journalistic practice reflect the need to deal with this tension.

While the function of news sources as primary definers of events, and the cultural and ideological ramifications of this practice, have attracted some scholarly interest (e.g., Hall et al. 1978; Reese 1990), their function as agents of legitimation and authority building has been studied much less. Still, the processes and practices of mutual legitimation between journalists and their sources, which this book addresses, bear significant implications for the authority of journalists, the produced news, and the legitimation of hegemonic power in society.

In order to study these processes of inter- and intra-legitimation, and their ideological dimensions, a framework for identifying discourses of legitimation in the news was developed. This framework profits from the analytical toolbox of critical discourse analysis and Norman Fairclough's (1992, 2015) approach to discourse and power, combined with a cultural studies approach to journalistic authority and narrative (Zelizer 1992, 2004).

This study moves beyond a narrowly focussed micro-textual approach in order to identify discourse not only as language but also as practice (performed also through language). The examination of discourses of legitimation (as they are put into practice by the professional norms and are crystallised in the produced news) through the prism of the dual logic of news, as facts and as stories, allows us to highlight the professional, cultural, and ideological dimensions of legitimation. Also, the special focus on news sources makes it possible to investigate the complex processes of mutual authority building and confirmation, between journalists and their sources, and how they enhance each side's status, legitimacy, and power.

The book starts by providing in Chapter 1 a concise overview of the constituents of the economic crisis and the political system in Greece, to allow for this research to be embedded in its socio-political context. It then gives in Chapter 2 a short description of the media environment in Greece, with a special focus on the two newspapers studied and on the news media representations of the economic crisis in the country, to assist the contextualisation of the study in its mediated environment and related journalistic practices.

The book moves then to introduce and discuss in a detailed fashion in Chapter 3 the components and dimensions of the analytical model for the identification of legitimation discourse, addressing their conceptual and theoretical foundations. The developed model, adopting a meso–macro textual and contextual approach to discourse, incorporates the examination of legitimation discourse through the prism of the factual/narrative logic of news, examined in three interrelated areas: (a) the systematic analysis of news texts focussing on the presence of news sources, (b) the analysis of the journalistic practices that relate to the construction of these news texts, and (c) the contextualisation of the analysis in its specific socio-political environment. This chapter gives also a brief account of the research methods employed, the empirical material, and the analytical process.

Chapter 4 focusses on the presentation of the research findings, by putting the developed analytical framework into use. The analysis of crisis-related news published in the Greek newspapers *Ta Nea* and *I Kathimerini* identified two overarching discourses of legitimation – objectivation and naturalisation – which relate to the dual factual/narrative logic of news. This chapter explains how the two discourses and their mechanisms are used to legitimate or delegitimate the authority positions of the involved actors and of journalists themselves, and validate the hegemonic ideologies over the economic crisis and its handling.

The concluding chapter reflects on the main research findings, on the appropriateness of its theoretical-analytical approach, and on the study's limitations. This chapter ends with a discussion on what the implications of the research findings are for journalism in Greece, in conditions of a prolonged (economic) crisis, media and journalism impoverishment, and high antagonism in socio-political life.

References

Berkowitz, Dan. 2009. "Reporters and Their Sources." In *The Handbook of Journalism Studies*, edited by Karin Wahl-Jorgensen and Thomas Hanitzsch, 102–15. New York: Routledge.

Coombs, W. Timothy. 2015. *Ongoing Crisis Communication: Planning, Managing, and Responding*. 4th ed. Thousand Oaks, CA: Sage.

Doudaki, Vaia. 2018. "Discourses of Legitimation in the News: The Case of the Cypriot Bailout." In *Cyprus and Its Conflicts: Representations, Materialities and Cultures*, edited by Vaia Doudaki and Nico Carpentier, 142–62. New York: Berghahn Books.

Doudaki, Vaia, Angeliki Boubouka, Lia-Paschalia Spyridou, and Christos Tzalavras. 2016. "Dependency, (Non)Liability and Austerity News Frames of Bailout Greece." *European Journal of Communication* 31 (4): 426–45.

Doudaki, Vaia, Angeliki Boubouka, and Christos Tzalavras. 2019. "Framing the Cypriot Financial Crisis: In the Service of the Neoliberal Vision." *Journalism* 20 (2): 349–68.

Doudaki, Vaia, and Nico Carpentier. 2018. "Introduction: A Multidisciplinary and Multiperspectival Approach to Conflict." In *Cyprus and Its Conflicts: Representations, Materialities and Cultures*, edited by Vaia Doudaki and Nico Carpentier, 1–21. New York: Berghahn Books.

Entman, Robert M. 2004. *Projections of Power: Framing News, Public Opinion, and US Foreign Policy*. Chicago: University of Chicago Press.

Fairclough, Norman. 1992. *Discourse and Social Change*. Cambridge: Polity Press.
Fairclough, Norman. 2015. *Language and Power*. 3rd ed. New York: Routledge.
Gitlin, Todd. 1980. *The Whole World Is Watching: Mass Media in the Making and Unmaking of the New Left*. Berkeley: University of California Press.
Hall, Stuart, Chas Critcher, Tony Jefferson, John Clarke, and Brian Roberts. 1978. *Policing the Crisis: Mugging, the State, and Law and Order*. New York: Palgrave Macmillan.
Reese, Stephen D. 1990. "The News Paradigm and the Ideology of Objectivity: A Socialist at the Wall Street Journal." *Critical Studies in Media Communication* 7 (4): 390–409.
Reshef, Yonatan, and Charles Keim. 2014. *Bad Time Stories: Government-Union Conflicts and the Rhetoric of Legitimation Strategies*. Toronto: University of Toronto Press.
Tuchman, Gaye. 1978. *Making News: A Study in the Construction of Reality*. New York: Free Press.
Vaara, Eero. 2014. "Struggles over Legitimacy in the Eurozone Crisis: Discursive Legitimation Strategies and Their Ideological Underpinnings." *Discourse & Society* 25 (4): 500–18.
Vaara, Eero, and Janne Tienari. 2008. "A Discursive Perspective on Legitimation Strategies in Multinational Corporations." *Academy of Management Review* 33 (4): 985–93.
Vecchi, Gregory M. 2009. "Conflict and Crisis Communication." *Annals of the American Psychotherapy Association* 12 (1): 34–42.
Zelizer, Barbie. 1992. *Covering the Body: The Kennedy Assassination, the Media, and the Shaping of Collective Memory*. Chicago: University of Chicago Press.
Zelizer, Barbie. 2004. "When Facts, Truth, and Reality Are God-Terms: On Journalism's Uneasy Place in Cultural Studies." *Communication and Critical/Cultural Studies* 1 (1): 100–19.

1 The economic crisis in Greece

Short account of events and actors

Angeliki Boubouka

What has been known as the recession of 2008–2009, which was caused by a global credit crunch, affected the European countries in varying degrees, with the southern periphery being more vulnerable, due to high debts (Myant et al. 2016, 7–8). At first, European governments responded to recession moderately, by enacting policies that aimed at guaranteeing social protection whilst re-establishing financial stability and stimulating economic demand (The World Bank 2011, 82). However, soon after, they prioritised the protection of the financial system, following policies focussed on the reduction of state debts and on economic growth through deregulation. From 2010 onward, crisis-hit countries adopted more aggressive strategies, including austerity measures, such as contractionary fiscal policies, and cuts in public spending, pension reforms, and labour rights, in order to (re)gain the confidence of financial markets (Council of Europe 2013, 13).

The Greek economy has traditionally been characterised by state-driven development, a dysfunctional public sector, clientelism (Featherstone 2011, 2015), and particularly high pervasiveness of party patronage "used both as a tool of (policy) control (at the top) and of (electoral) reward (at the bottom)" (Afonso et al. 2015, 320), leading to selective distribution of state resources to serve the party clientele. This situation did not fundamentally change after Greece joined the single currency (euro). Instead, the endemic weaknesses of the Greek economy intensified its lack of competitiveness, fuelled also by the structural asymmetries within the Eurozone. Greece was thus already heavily indebted, in 2009, due to its state-driven expansion and debt-driven growth (Pagoulatos 2018, 1–4).

During the last quarter of 2009, Greece's capacity to continue servicing its debt became increasingly questionable, which was reflected also in the skyrocketing of its interest rates. During the following months, the recently elected socialist government of PASOK announced a series of austerity measures, in an effort to reduce the country's public debt and curtail its deficit.[1] In April 2010 the borrowing costs for Greece reached "unsustainable levels" according to the EU (ESM 2018). Prime Minister George Papandreou asked for the activation of a bailout package from the EU and the IMF. In May, the Eurogroup approved a three-year joint financial assistance programme for Greece, through bilateral loans provided by Eurozone countries (€80 billion) and the IMF (€30 billion), in order "to safeguard financial stability in the euro area as a whole" (Eurogroup 2010). In June, the Eurozone member states established the European Financial Stability Facility (EFSF) (ESM n.d.a), a temporary bailout fund created to provide financial assistance to Eurozone states in economic difficulty.

Following the deal, the Greek government announced new, stricter austerity measures, causing waves of protest across the country. The creditors' requirements entailed a state of emergency, invoked by all the Greek governments from then on, in the name of national interest, in order to pass and apply harsh legislation, often through shrinking or by-passing legislative procedures (Papavlassopoulos 2015, 158). Austerity aimed at reducing government spending and at reforms that "include the removal of labour market rigidities, increasing their tax-collecting capacity, and making significant changes to retirement ages, in particular for public-sector workers", as well as "cutting state pension benefits and public-sector wages" (Kelsey et al. 2016, 5). Despite the bailout deal, the recession deepened, financial indicators worsened, social unrest spread, and financial markets showed further distrust towards Greece. In October 2011, there were talks for a second bailout as the Greek side admitted it could not meet the 2011 and 2012 deficit targets agreed with the EU and the IMF, due to the much deeper-than-predicted recession.

In late October, the Eurozone leaders reached an initial agreement for new bailout loans (€130 billion), in return for new austerity measures, accompanied by a 50% "haircut" of Greece's debt to the private sector: Private investors holding Greek bonds were invited to develop a voluntary bond exchange with a nominal discount (haircut) of 50% – which later reached 53.5% (Eurogroup 2012) – facilitating a €100 billion debt reduction for Greece (European Commission n.d.). The haircut scenario had been dismissed by EU officials back in 2009 as an "inconsiderable option". Prime Minister George Papandreou proposed a referendum on the new financial assistance programme, causing intense reactions among creditors and domestic political actors, who wanted to avoid the risk of an agreement rejection and potential political instability.

The proposed referendum was cancelled, but the proposal had already initiated a domino effect of political events that led to Papandreou's resignation and the formation of a coalition government. Three parties – the socialist PASOK, centre-right-wing New Democracy, and nationalist LAOS – formed a transitory government of "national unity" in order to pave the way for the new bailout, appointing the erstwhile vice-president of the European Central Bank (ECB), Loukas Papademos, as the new Prime Minister, on 11 November. The second Memorandum was voted upon by the Greek parliament in February 2012, despite massive protests and disapproval by members of the governmental parties. One month later, it was approved by the Eurogroup, which agreed that the EFSF would "provide an additional €130 billion to help Greece meet its financing needs" (European Commission n.d.). The IMF agreed to contribute an additional €19.8 billion.

The double 2012 elections that followed revealed major shifts in the voting behaviour of Greeks and introduced a new political landscape in the country. The first election results, of 6 May, were interpreted as the voters' punishment against the political parties that supported Memoranda and austerity measures. PASOK and New Democracy, which had dominated the domestic political scene the past 40 years, lost more than 60% of their voting power, despite New Democracy's first-place position with 18.9%.[2] Syriza (a coalition party of left, radical left, and green groups), led by Alexis Tsipras, was second with 16.6%.

Fruitless efforts to form a coalition government led to a second round of elections on 17 June. New Democracy got 29.53% of the vote and Syriza 27.12%.[3] A new coalition government, under Prime Minister Antonis Samaras, was formed by New Democracy, PASOK (13.18% of the vote), and the Democratic Left (6.11%) with the assertion that it would renegotiate the loan agreements with the Troika. Meanwhile, previous Memoranda requirements, including a series of salaries and pension cuts, were being implemented.

Among other shifts during the 2012 elections, the neo-Nazi party Golden Dawn attracted 7% of the vote in both rounds and entered Parliament, signifying the first parliamentary presence of the extreme right since the fall of dictatorship in 1974. These elections revealed a new pro-Memorandum–anti-Memorandum axis dividing the Greek political landscape, which is different than, and intersecting, the traditional left–right axis (Katsanidou 2015, 69).

In October 2012, Eurozone members created the European Stability Mechanism, a Eurozone-wide crisis fighting mechanism, as an additional tool to the EFSF. This was funded with €80 billion by its members, including Greece (ESM n.d.a). In November, the Troika (EU, ECB, IMF) agreed on a series of debt facilitation measures for Greece, aiming to reduce Greece's debt to 124% of GDP by 2020 (ESM n.d.b). At the same time, Troika representatives regularly reviewed the implementation of the agreed-upon measures, increasing the pressure for compliance with the bailout terms, whenever fiscal targets were not met. Among the measures implemented during 2012 was a 22% minimum wage reduction, which affected all collective labour agreements and caused further recession. That, combined with growing unemployment, led to a mass reduction of government revenue from taxes and social insurance contributions (Malkoutzis and Mouzakis 2015).

In addition, attempted reforms in public administration turned out to be inapplicable or unsuccessful given the differences of the promoted Anglo-Saxon model, which prioritises financial management, audit and efficiency, and the domestic administrative culture of party-statism, clientelism, and centralised bureaucracy (Featherstone 2015), as well as the disturbance of the power dynamics among domestic elites (Zahariadis 2013). For example, the emergence of political parties such as the neo-Nazi Golden Dawn and populist right Independent Greeks, during this period, is attributed, inter alia, to their ability to attract voters who favour state interventionism and social conservatism and were not represented by existing parties (Katsanidou 2015, 69).

As the crisis deepened, EU officials were impeached for imposing growth models that did not fit the economies of crisis-hit countries of southern Europe, such as Greece, by "seeking a single set of 'best practices' deemed applicable to all economies", instead of "finding a successful national path [which] requires adapting social and economic policies to the institutional conditions specific to each type of political economy" (Hall 2018, 25). In June 2013, the IMF admitted that its 2010 forecast (IMF 2010) for the Greek economy had been too optimistic and that it had underestimated the damage that austerity measures would do to the Greek economy (IMF 2013). For example, the IMF's projection referred to a decline in unemployment to 15% during 2012 – when it reached 25% before peaking at 27.9% (58.3% for people below the age of 25) in July 2013.[4] The 2013 IMF report referred to the 2010–2012 bailout programme as a "holding operation" that gave the Eurozone and the global economy "time to build a firewall to protect other vulnerable members and averted potentially severe effects on the global economy" (IMF 2013, 28). Among the admitted failures of the first bailout programme was the fact that confidence in the financial markets was not restored, the banking system lost 30% of its deposits, and the Greek economy experienced a much deeper-than-expected recession. In a 2018 review, the IMF admitted that the delay in debt restructuring in Greece had actually benefited European banks by giving them time to dispose of Greek bonds (IMF 2019).

In 2014 the Greek economy showed some signs of growth, while the cumulative loss of real GDP over the period 2010–2016 reached nearly 25%, mainly due to the collapse of internal demand (Argitis et al. 2017, 13). In December 2014, the Greek parliament failed to reach the majority required for the election of the President of Greece, leading to snap national elections on 25 January 2015. The left-wing Syriza won (36.34%)[5] on an anti-bailout agenda and formed a coalition government with the populist-right party of

Independent Greeks, with the primary aim to renegotiate the Greek debt and tackle the "humanitarian crisis" the country was facing.

The new government froze the implementation of some of the agreed-upon reforms (privatisations, wage cuts, etc.) while Yanis Varoufakis, the new Finance Minister, attempted to convince the creditors to negotiate a new agreement, which would include a combination of fiscal targets and reforms that would limit austerity and reduce Greece's fiscal "suffocation". The second bailout programme ended on 28 February, and the government worked to achieve a bridging deal that would allow the ECB to continue funding Greek banks until the new agreement was reached. In March, Greece secured a four-month extension of the programme, under the condition that it would stick to the agreed reforms, as Germany-led partners insisted. During this period, deposits fled from Greek banks and ECB provided emergency funding to keep the banking system operating. Greece struggled to stick to its debt repayments to the IMF. The creditors were openly referring to the possibility of a "Grexit" (Greek exit) from the Eurozone (Ekathimerini.com 2015).

In June, Greece submitted a new reform plan, but negotiations became stuck over disagreements with the creditors, mainly regarding labour market and pension reforms. The IMF withdrew from the talks a few days before the programme extension expired, with Greece being at risk of defaulting on its (€320 billion) loans. The EU accused the Tsipras government of lying and not compromising. On 25 June, under the creditors' pressure to accept a new austerity package, Tsipras rejected a five-month extension of the bailout programme; the next day, he called for a referendum on the creditors' proposal. This was scheduled to take place on 5 July. On 28 June, capital controls (controls on bank transfers from Greek banks to foreign banks, and limits on cash withdrawals) were imposed, and it was decided that banks would stay closed until 7 July, in order to avoid a financial panic. On 30 June, Greece defaulted on its creditors, failing to repay a €1.5 billion instalment to the IMF (IMF 2015), while the EFSF bailout programme expired (ESM 2015).

Amidst acute political polarisation, and Prime Minister Tsipras framing the referendum as a choice between the anti-Memorandum government and the "restoration" of the old political system (Chryssogelos 2017, 481), Greek voters rejected the creditors' package proposal, by 61.31% of the vote.[6] The creditors, who interpreted the referendum as a choice between the euro and the drachma (Greece's currency before joining the Eurozone), set a deadline of 12 July for Tsipras to compromise on the proposed cuts and reforms, with the warning that the alternative would be expulsion from the Eurozone.

After a heated emergency EU–IMF summit, Greece agreed to a third bailout agreement, containing tough austerity measures, privatisations, and reforms, in return for €86 billion of financial support and the promise of future debt restructuring. Banks reopened on 17 July. The agreement was backed by a large parliamentary majority in August, and then approved by ESM, but Syriza faced left-wing dissidents. Tsipras called for early elections on 20 September 2015 and won the majority of the vote (35.46%).[7]

During 2015 and 2016 the Greek economy remained weak and stagnant (Argitis et al. 2017, 13), while in 2017 some signs of stabilisation started to appear. In June 2018, the Eurogroup confirmed that Greece would be ready in August to complete the third programme requirements, and it agreed on mid-term debt facilitation measures. Despite the "clean exit" government assertion, creditors required the activation of an enhanced surveillance framework to secure the implementation of the agreed reforms (Ekathimerini.com 2018a). According to the post-bailout framework, Greece has to achieve high primary budget surpluses of above 3.5% through 2022. Regular budget monitoring is scheduled to be carried out until 75% of the bailout debt is repaid (Ekathimerini.com 2018b).

The Bank of Greece (BoG), in its Monetary Policy Report 2017–2018 (Bank of Greece 2018) estimated that "primary surpluses of 3.5% of GDP until 2022 and 2.2% of GDP on average in the period from 2023 to 2060", would be an infeasible target. "No other country in the world, with the possible exception of oil producing countries, has ever achieved such large primary surpluses over such a protracted period", the report stressed. As noted in the report, "this assumption [. . .] constitutes the greatest risk in the analysis of long-term debt sustainability", warning that such large primary surpluses will "burden future generations".

In 2018, the primary budget surplus exceeded the set target, reaching 4.4% of GDP (Ana.gr 2019), which was interpreted by the parties of the opposition, and by the business sector, as the result of increased taxes combined with severe cuts in state spending and public investments (Naftemporiki.gr 2018), suffocating the real economy and undermining growth. Tsipras government, in constrast, saw the surpluses as an opportunity to enact social policy by offering tax-breaks and welfare spending (Naftemporiki.gr 2019).

Overall, the economic programmes implemented in Greece as part of the bailout agreements have been critiqued as not supporting real growth while deregulating the labour market and undermining the welfare state (Robolis 2015). In practice, high unemployment – combined with the loosening of the employment protection legislation while the real economy was in free fall – intensified the effects of recession, which turned into a depression.

The impact of austerity is depicted in the EU SILC index,[8] concerning the living conditions among the population: In 2016 the percentage of severely materially deprived persons in the country peaked at 22.4% of the population, almost double than in 2010 (11.6%). Also, during 2014–2017 at least

Table 1.1 The Greek economy in numbers[9]

	2008	*2009*	*2010*	*2011*	*2012*	*2013*	*2014*	*2015*	*2016*	*2017*	*2018*
Real GDP growth rate*	−0.3	−4.3	−5.5	−9.1p**	−7.3p	−3.2p	0.7p	−0.4p	−0.2p	1.5p	1.9p
GDP (bl euro)	264.775	301.062	330.570	356.235	305.085	320.498	319.629	311.729	315.010	317.485	334.573
General government gross debt (% of GDP)	109.4	126.7	146.2	172.1	159.6	177.4	178.9	175.9	178.5	176.2	181.1
General government gross debt (bl euro)	264.775	301.062	330.570	356.235	305.085	320.498	319.629	311.729	315.010	317.485	334.573
Government deficit/ surplus (% of GDP)	–	−15.1	−11.2	−10.3	−8.9	−13.2	−3.6	−5.6	0.5	0.7	1.1
Unemployment rate	7.8	9.6	12.7	17.9	24.5	27.5	26.5	24.9	23.6	21.5	19.3
Ten-year government bond yield, average	4.8	5.17	9.09	15.75	22.5	10.05	6.93	9.67	8.36	5.98	–

* Percentage change on previous year

** p = provisional

one in three residents of Greece was at risk of poverty or social exclusion, while the EU-28 average was fewer than one in four people (ELSTAT 2019).

In November 2018 Greece still recorded the highest unemployment rate in the EU and the Eurozone (18.5% of total population, 39.1% in ages under 25).[10] Despite the drop of unemployment since its peak in 2013, 2018 was the fifth year in the row with over one million unemployed people. In addition, most of the new jobs were part-time. In the period 2013–2017, involuntarily temporary employees reached 72% (ETUC and ETUI 2018, 26). More than 54.3% of recruitments in 2018 were for temporary jobs (in comparison to 21% in 2009), while salaries dropped significantly: In 2018 50% of employees in the private sector earned less than €793 per month (depicting a 30% loss in employee income during 2010–2018) (INE GSEE 2019).

During 2010–2016, more than 350,000 Greek citizens, mainly 26–40 years old (Iliopoulou 2016), migrated abroad (New Diaspora 2019). According to the BoG, on a cumulative basis, during 2008–2013, 427,000 Greek residents (in a country of 10.8 million) left the country permanently (ELSTAT 2019). It was the first emigration outflow in Greek history of primarily educated people with work experience (mainly headed for Germany, the UK, and the United Arab Emirates) in comparison to the unskilled, low-educated workers who had emigrated in the past (Lazaretou 2016).

Among the profound effects of the crisis has also been the downgrading of basic human rights and democratic standards. The rights of work, health, housing, and education have been reported as being undermined and violated under the austerity regime in Greece. According to the International Federation of Human Rights 2014 report, "[t]he complex institutional set-up behind the so-called 'Troika' has served as a smokescreen shielding its constituents from responsibility for human rights violations for too long" (FIDG and Hellenic League for Human Rights 2014, 68), while the EU Member States breached their obligations to assist Greece in fulfilling its human rights commitments, "by setting up the Troika and endorsing its proposals" (ibid., 69).

Notes

1 For Greece's macroeconomic data during 2008–2018, see Table 1.1.
2 Source: Ministry of Interior of Greece. http://ekloges-prev.singularlogic.eu/v2012a/public/index.html
3 Source: Ministry of Interior of Greece. http://ekloges-prev.singularlogic.eu/v2012b/public/index.html?lang=en
4 Source: Eurostat. https://ec.europa.eu/eurostat/tgm/table.do?tab=table&init=1&plugin=1&pcode=tipsun20&language=en
5 Source: Ministry of Interior of Greece. http://ekloges-prev.singularlogic.eu/v2015a/v/public/index.html

6 Source: Ministry of Interior of Greece. http://ekloges-prev.singularlogic.eu/r2015/e/public/index.html
7 Source: Ministry of Interior of Greece. http://ekloges-prev.singularlogic.eu/v2015b/v/public/index.html
8 Source: Eurostat. https://ec.europa.eu/eurostat/tgm/table.do?tab=table&init=1&plugin=1&pcode=tipslc30&language=en.
9 Sources: Eurostat. https://ec.europa.eu/eurostat/web/products-datasets. OECD, Long-term interest rates (indicator). doi: 10.1787/662d712c-en.
10 Source: Eurostat. https://ec.europa.eu/eurostat/statistics-explained/index.php/Unemployment_statistics#Longer-term_unemployment_trends.

References

Afonso, Alexandre, Sotirios Zartaloudis, and Yannis Papadopoulos. 2015. "How Party Linkages Shape Austerity Politics: Clientelism and Fiscal Adjustment in Greece and Portugal during the Eurozone Crisis." *Journal of European Public Policy* 22 (3): 315–34.

Ana.gr. 2019. "Greek Budget Showed a Primary Surplus of 4.4 Pct of GDP in 2018." 23 April. www.ana.gr/en/article/354862/.

Argitis, Giorgos, Nasos Koratzanis, and Christos Pierros. 2017. "The Greek Crisis: Outlook and an Alternative Economic Policy." In *iAGS 2017 The Elusive Recovery: Special Studies on Greece and Germany*, 5–50. www.socialistsanddemocrats.eu/sites/default/files/iAGS%202017%20THE%20ELUSIVE%20RECOVERY%20-%20Special%20studies%20on%20Greece%20and%20Germany%204_1.pdf.

Bank of Greece. 2018. "Monetary Policy Report 2017–2018." Press Release. www.bankofgreece.gr/pages/en/bank/news/pressreleases/DispItem.aspx?Item_ID=6112&List_ID=1af869f3-57fb-4de6-b9ae-bdfd83c66c95&Filter_by=DT.

Chryssogelos, Angelos. 2017. "The People in the 'Here and Now': Populism, Modernization and the State in Greece." *International Political Science Review* 38 (4): 473–87.

Council of Europe. 2013. *Safeguarding Human Rights in Times of Economic Crisis*. Issue Paper. Commissioner for Human Rights. https://rm.coe.int/safeguarding-human-rights-in-times-of-economic-crisis-issue-paper-publ/1680908dfa.

Ekathimerini.com. 2015. "Moscovici Warns 'Grexit Could Be Beginning of the End' in Der Spiegel." 13 March. www.ekathimerini.com/168206/article/ekathimerini/business/moscovici-warns-grexit-could-be-beginning-of-the-end-in-der-spiegel.

Ekathimerini.com. 2018a. "Commission Confirms Adoption of Enhanced Surveillance Framework for Greece." 11 July. www.ekathimerini.com/230567/article/ekathimerini/business/commission-confirms-adoption-of-enhanced-surveillance-framework-for-greece.

Ekathimerini.com. 2018b. "Creditors Say Greece Will Get Tough Monitoring after Bailout." July 11. www.ekathimerini.com/230568/article/ekathimerini/business/creditors-say-greece-will-get-tough-monitoring-after-bailout.

ELSTAT. 2019. *Greece in Figures: January–March 2019*. Hellenic Statistical Authority. www.statistics.gr/documents/20181/1515741/GreeceInFigures_2019Q1_EN.pdf/31e71c09-7bf3-4695-a410-eaefe07532ca.

ESM. 2015. "EFSF Programme for Greece Expires Today." ESM Press Release, 30 June. www.esm.europa.eu/press-releases/efsf-programme-greece-expires-today.

ESM. 2018. "Timeline of Events: 2009–2018." 20 August. www.esm.europa.eu/assistance/greece/timeline-greece-exit.

ESM. n.d.a. "History." Accessed 4 May 2019. www.esm.europa.eu/about-us/history.

ESM. n.d.b. Financial Assistance to Greece. Accessed 20 July 2019. https://ec.europa.eu/info/business-economy-euro/economic-and-fiscal-policy-coordination/eu-financial-assistance/which-eu-countries-have-received-assistance/financial-assistance-greece_en#secondeconomicadjustmentprogrammeforgreece.

ETUC and ETUI. 2018. "Labour Market and Social Developments." In *Benchmarking Working Europe 2018*, 19–35. European Trade Union Institute. www.etui.org/Publications2/Books/Benchmarking-Working-Europe-2018.

Eurogroup. 2010. "Statement by the Eurogroup." 2 May. www.consilium.europa.eu/media/25673/20100502-eurogroup_statement_greece.pdf.

Eurogroup. 2012. "Eurogroup Statement." 21 February. www.esm.europa.eu/sites/default/files/2012-02-21_eurogroup_statement_bailout_for_greece.pdf.

European Commission. n.d. "A New Chapter for Greece: Timeline of Events." Accessed 4 May 2019. https://ec.europa.eu/info/sites/info/files/economy-finance/05_timeline_of_events_2.pdf.

Featherstone, Kevin. 2011. "The JCMS Annual Lecture: The Greek Sovereign Debt Crisis and EMU: A Failing State in a Skewed Regime." *JCMS: Journal of Common Market Studies* 49 (2): 193–217.

Featherstone, Kevin. 2015. "External Conditionality and the Debt Crisis: The 'Troika' and Public Administration Reform in Greece." *Journal of European Public Policy* 22 (3): 295–314.

FIDG and Hellenic League for Human Rights. 2014. *Downgrading Rights: The Cost of Austerity in Greece*. www.fidh.org/IMG/pdf/downgrading_rights_the_cost_of_austerity_in_greece.pdf.

Hall, Peter A. 2018. "Varieties of Capitalism in Light of the Euro Crisis." *Journal of European Public Policy* 25 (1): 7–30.

Iliopoulou, Galini. 2016. "Young Talented Greeks Working Abroad." In *Performance Management from Drain to Gain.* ICAP presentation, 2nd Human Capital Summit. 4 May. http://dir.icap.gr/mailimages/Young%20Talented%20Greeks%20abroad%20presentation_Galini%20Iliopoulou.pdf.

IMF. 2010. *Greece: Staff Report on Request for Stand-By Arrangement*. IMF Country Report No. 10/110, May. www.imf.org/external/pubs/ft/scr/2010/cr10110.pdf.

IMF. 2013. *Greece: Ex Post Evaluation of Exceptional Access under the 2010 Stand-By Arrangement*. IMF Country Report No. 13/156, June. www.imf.org/external/pubs/ft/scr/2013/cr13156.pdf.

IMF. 2015. *Press Release: Statement by the IMF on Greece*. IMF Press Release No. 15/310, 30 June. www.imf.org/en/News/Articles/2015/09/14/01/49/pr15310.

IMF. 2019. *2018 Review of Program Design and Conditionality*. IMF Policy Paper No. 19/012, May. www.imf.org/en/Publications/Policy-Papers/Issues/2019/05/20/2018-Review-of-Program-Design-and-Conditionality-46910.

INE GSEE. 2019. *Η Ελληνική Οικονομία και η Απασχόληση. Ετήσια Έκθεση 2019 [The Greek Economy and Employment. Annual Report 2019]*. Institute of Employment GSEE. www.inegsee.gr/wp-content/uploads/2019/05/Etisia_Ekthesi_2019_H_Elliniki_Oikonomia_kai_i_Apasxolisi.pdf.

Katsanidou, Alexia. 2015. "Η Τοποθέτηση των Πολιτών στον Άξονα Αριστεράς-Δεξιάς: Η Σημασία και το Περιεχόμενο [The Positioning of Citizens on the Left-Right Axis: Meaning and Context]." In *Το Πολιτικό Πορτραίτο της Ελλάδας [The Political Portrait of Greece]*, edited by Nikos G. Georgarakis and Nicolas Demertzis, 51–74. Athens: Gutenberg Editions and National Centre for Social Research.

Kelsey, Darren, Frank Mueller, Andrea Whittle, and Majid KhosraviNik. 2016. "Financial Crisis and Austerity: Interdisciplinary Concerns in Critical Discourse Studies." *Critical Discourse Studies* 13 (1): 1–19.

Lazaretou, Sophia. 2016. "The Greek Brain Drain: The New Pattern of Greek Emigration during the Recent Crisis." In *Bank of Greece: Economic Bulletin No. 43*, 31–54. Bank of Greece. www.bankofgreece.gr/BogEkdoseis/econbull201607.pdf.

Malkoutzis, Nick and Yiannis Mouzakis. 2015. "You've Heard the Greek Crisis Myths, Now Here Are Some Truths." *Macropolis.gr*, 20 February. http://www.macropolis.gr/?i=portal.en.the-agora.2268.

Myant, Martin, Sotiria Theodoropoulou, and Agnieszka Piasna. 2016. "Introduction." In *Unemployment, Internal Devaluation and Labour Market Deregulation in Europe*. Brussels: European Trade Union Institute. www.etui.org/Publications2/Books/Unemployment-internal-devaluation-and-labour-market-deregulation-in-Europe.

Naftemporiki.gr. 2018. "Massive 7.6 bln € Greek Primary Budget Surplus in Jan-Nov Generated by Taxes, Spending and Investments Cuts." 15 December. www.naftemporiki.gr/story/1424638/massive-76-bln-greek-primary-budget-surplus-in-Jan-nov-generated-by-taxes-spending-and-investments-cuts.

Naftemporiki.gr. 2019. "Trailing Tsipras Govt Eyes Money from Massive Primary Budget Surplus for Tax Breaks, Welfare Spending." 24 April. www.naftemporiki.gr/story/1469114/trailing-tsipras-govt-eyes-money-from-massive-primary-budget-surplus-for-tax-breaks-welfare-spending.

New Diaspora. 2019. "The Number of Greeks Who Moved Abroad during the Crisis." 4 May. www.newdiaspora.com/the-number-of-greeks-who-moved-abroad-during-the-crisis/.

Pagoulatos, George. 2018. *Greece after the Bailouts: Assessment of a Qualified Failure*. GreeSE Paper No. 130. Hellenic Observatory Papers on Greece and Southeast Europe. www.lse.ac.uk/Hellenic-Observatory/Assets/Documents/Publications/GreeSE-Papers/GreeSE-No130.pdf.

Papavlassopoulos, Efthimis. 2015. "Μετατοπίσεις στο Ελληνικό Κομματικό Σύστημα: Από το Ενιαίο Μαζικό Κόμμα του Κράτους στο κόμμα 'Εκτάκτου Εθνικής Ανάγκης' [Transformations and Shifts in the Greek Party System: From the Mass Party of the State to the 'National Emergency Party'?]." In *Το Πολιτικό Πορτραίτο της Ελλάδας [The Political Portrait of Greece]*, edited by Nikos G. Georgarakis and Nicolas Demertzis, 141–67. Athens: Gutenberg Editions and National Centre for Social Research.

Robolis, Savvas G. 2015. "Οικονομική Κρίση και Κράτος Πρόνοιας [Economic Crisis and the Welfare State]." In *Το Πολιτικό Πορτραίτο της Ελλάδας [The*

Political Portrait of Greece], edited by Nikos G. Georgarakis and Nicolas Demertzis, 378–91. Athens: Gutenberg Editions and National Centre for Social Research.

The World Bank. 2011. *The Jobs Crisis: Household and Government Responses to the Great Recession in Eastern Europe and Central Asia.* http://documents.worldbank.org/curated/en/793341468252626562/pdf/608090PUB0Jobs10Box358332B01PUBLIC1.pdf.

Zahariadis, Nikolaos. 2013. "Leading Reform Amidst Transboundary Crises: Lessons from Greece." *Public Administration* 91 (3): 648–62.

2 Media and representations of the economic crisis

Angeliki Boubouka and Vaia Doudaki

The media in Greece (in times of crisis)

The media in Greece, and press in particular, has historically been distinguished through its close affiliations with the political system, seen as reflecting the Mediterranean or polarised pluralist media system model (Hallin and Mancini 2004). This model, found in countries of the (European) South, is characterised inter alia by a tradition in commentary-oriented journalism, late development of press freedom and of media commercialisation, and relatively low newspaper readership and sales. Even after state monopoly over radio and television was abolished in Greece, starting in late 1980s, and the press entered an era of commercialisation, "the overpoliticization of the press and the heavy dependence of both broadcast and print media upon state resources for their survival" (Papatheodorou and Machin 2003, 32) continued to shape the country's media landscape.

The political patronage and pressure for political support that is typical of this entanglement is related to, for example, the decades-long delay of broadcast license awarding, provision of loans to media companies in privileged terms, debt and fine write-offs, subsidies through state advertising (often to newspapers with minimal circulation), and the "appointment of leading editorial personnel from large media groups to important public posts" (Papatheodorou and Machin 2003, 50) – all which have created an environment of mutual benefits between governments, political parties, and media (Papathanassopoulos 2004). The significance of this entanglement is enhanced by the fact that a number of media companies gradually moved into the hands of businessmen with activities in various sectors (constructions, telecommunications, etc.). The owners of these companies would use the media they controlled to gain privileged contracts with the public sector by offering favourable political coverage (ibid., 148–57).

Not surprisingly, given its inherent weaknesses, the media sector in Greece has been highly affected by the economic crisis. Unemployment among media workers, which was reported to be lower than the country's average before the crisis, exploded after 2010 and peaked to 39% in 2014, due to the closure of some of the largest legacy media organisations. By 2016, sectoral unemployment fell to 12%, only to rise again in 2018, to 15.5% (Kapsalis 2018, 22).

The effects of the economic crisis entrapped media companies in an endless circle of debts, operational shrinkage, circulation and advertising losses, bankruptcies, etc. In 2013 the four remaining large media organisations were heavily in debt (Darzanou 2013). Since then, only one – *I Kathimerini* – has avoided closure or takeover. Media companies followed cost-reduction strategies that included layoffs, pay cuts, outlet closures, and replacement of experienced, high-salaried journalists with younger low-cost professionals, on a large scale. Overall, the increase of temporary, undeclared, and precarious jobs, with limited – if any – social security coverage, underlines the deregulation of journalism (Kapsalis 2018, 25).

At the same time, the print media market shrunk dramatically. Although "[p]ublishers/media organizations want to hold on to the potential political influence that they can yield" there has been "considerable disinvestment from the field of media" (Siapera et al. 2015, 454). During the crisis, several new titles emerged, but most of them soon turned out to not be viable. In 2008, 22 Sunday newspapers sold 1,063,000 copies per week. In 2012, 16 papers sold 589,203 copies. Following the same trend, in 2018, 11 titles sold 144,462 copies (six newspapers have stopped publishing data about their sales) (Papachristoudi 2018). Yet, the print circulation shrinkage does not reflect a general phenomenon regarding all Greek media, argues Papathanassopoulos (2015, 457), since digital media keep emerging. According to the Online Media Registry of the Ministry of Digital Policy, in August 2017 there were more than 850 news websites, employing more than 7,600 journalists (Ministry of Digital Policy, Telecommunications and Media 2017). The large number of outlets, though, does not necessarily reflect journalistic pluralism. Since legacy and new media share a significantly reduced advertising expenditure (reduced by 65% in the years 2007–2013), there is little room for optimism regarding journalistic autonomy from "clientelistic relationships" that, as already mentioned, traditionally characterise the Greek media landscape (Papathanassopoulos 2015, 475).

It should be noted that Greek media, especially newspapers, are largely distrusted by citizens: radio and internet reached distrust rates of 37–38% in 2015, while television and newspapers distrust rates peaked at 77% in 2015 and 80% in 2014, respectively (Public Issue 2018). The grim picture is framed by concerns about media independence. Freedom of speech has been repeatedly challenged and undermined in Greece, as reported by various sources (e.g., Syllas 2013). According to the World Press Freedom Index (Reporters without Borders 2019), Greece had its worst performance in 2014, when it ranked 99th (among 180 countries), partly because of the Hellenic Broadcasting Corporation (ERT) closure in 2013 (it re-opened in 2015). During the next several years, Greece improved its position, ranking 65th in 2019, although in 2018 there were still concerns regarding incidents of lawsuits against journalists for defamation, restrictions of access to news events and to information, and assaults against reporters (Mapping Media Freedom 2019) – mostly during demonstrations and social unrest. In 2019, a landmark bill paved the way for the abolition of the "flagrant procedure" for press crimes that was frequently used by politicians and powerful businessmen to arrest journalists (Reporters without Borders 2019).

The two newspapers studied: *Ta Nea* and *I Kathimerini*

Our research focussed on two mainstream newspapers, *Ta Nea* (centre-left) and *I Kathimerini* (centre-right), selected by criteria of circulation and prominence among Greek media. They are both legacy outlets that were established in early 20th century. These newspapers represent two of the leading media organisations in the country and rank among the most popular newspapers, despite a circulation meltdown that occurred before and during the economic crisis.

Ta Nea (Τα Νέα, The News) was founded in 1931 (then called *Athinaika Nea*, Athenian News) by the Lambrakis Press Group (DOL), which was led by members of the Liberal Party. *Ta Nea* has historically played an interventionist role in the country's political developments. At the beginning of the economic crisis, DOL owned several print outlets, including the flagship newspapers *Ta Nea* and *To Vima*; one of the two Greek press distribution agencies, Argos (which was reported to the EU in 2019 for abusing its monopoly; Ana.gr 2019); one of the few domestic media printing companies; and several audio-visual media. DOL's leadership played a crucial role in supporting or undermining political actors at different times in contemporary Greek history – in a shadowy way in the distant past, and closer to front stage more recently (Psarras 2016).

DOL was among the media groups that collapsed during the economic crisis. As print sales and advertising spending dropped fast, deeply affecting all Greek media, it was unable to serve the huge bank loans that it had previously acquired with privileged terms (due to its close affiliation with the political system). In 2017, DOL suspended its operations and was sold at auction to Evangelos Marinakis, a shipping magnate who owned several print and online Greek media as well as sports teams in Greece and England. Until 2015 Marinakis had been president of Olympiakos football team (long-standing champion in Greece), but he was banned from sports involvement after being investigated for criminal cases of sports-match fixing, and drug smuggling (Keddie 2018).

Marinakis's media company, Alter Ego, currently owns most of the aforementioned ex-DOL media outlets, including *Ta Nea* (Naftemporiki.gr 2017). Since his involvement with media, Marinakis was referred to by the Syriza government as a prominent representative of the old, corrupt political and economic establishment and a "family friend" of New Democracy's leader, Kyriakos Mitsotakis (Ana.gr 2017). A few days before launching the Alter Ego internet TV station One, and while expecting a national broadcast license, Marinakis accused the Tsipras government of attempting to manipulate the 2016 broadcast license bidding process, in which he took part (Ekathimerini.com 2019).

The second newspaper of our study, *I Kathimerini* (Η Καθημερινή, The Daily), was founded in 1919 and run for decades by the Vlachos publishing family, as a broadsheet conservative daily. In 1987, due to economic difficulties, it was sold to a then-emerging banker, George Koskotas, who established one of the large media groups that characterised a new media era, and – like Marinakis – bought the Olympiakos football team and invested in several business sectors. Koskotas soon became the protagonist in a major political and economic corruption scandal that involved embezzling huge bank funds, bribing politicians, and taking control of several companies. Several politicians, including Prime Minister Andreas Papandreou, were taken to court (two former Ministers were convicted) in what was called at the time "the trial of the century" (1991–1992) in Greece (News247.gr 2014).

In 1988, Aristeidis Alafouzos, a former building constructor and member of a ship-owning family, bought *I Kathimerini* and created a media group. At the beginning of the economic crisis, the Alafouzos family was running Kathimerini Publishing S.A. and the Eidisis.com company, which owned the mainstream Skai TV/radio/news website. The family also owned or had shares in several other radio stations, news and sports websites, and a number of print media – some of which were shut down during the crisis (Smyrnaios 2008). Giannis Alafouzos, Aristeidis Alafouzos's son, became involved in Panathinaikos football team administration (holding the presidency from 2012 to 2017).

Under Alafouzos ownership, *I Kathimerini* has a liberal-conservative political orientation. The Syriza and Tsipras governments had controversial relations with the Alafouzos media group, mostly centering on Skai TV and radio. These media were boycotted by Syriza party/government politicians, first for a few days in 2015 (after the TV station hosted pro-"yes" guests the day before the 2015 referendum, thus violating a ban), and for a year starting in the summer of 2018 (following a critical report after the deadly Mati wildfire and ending before the July 2019 national elections, that brought New Democracy in power) (Naftemporiki.gr 2018; Thenationalherald.com 2019).

Representations of the crisis in the media

In its coverage of the economic crisis, domestic mainstream media largely "adopted the dominant ('pro-Memorandum') narrative of the crisis", in regard to its nature and its causes, as well as strategies for dealing with it (Pleios 2015, 520). The media did not contest Troika's neoliberal logic of defining the observed changes as a fiscal crisis, and blaming the country for increased state interventionism and for maintaining high social protection, but rather fostered it (ibid., 515). The domestic media promoted "the bail-outs' legitimation as 'necessity and fate' (Berger and Luckmann 1967, 91) for Greece's salvation, while selectively omitting or discrediting alternative voices and interpretations" (Doudaki 2015, 14).

The solutions proposed for tackling the crisis that appeared in the media favoured the dominant values of austerity and their supporting institutions (Serafis and Herman 2018, 196; Arrese 2018), echoing the neoliberal discourse (Mylonas 2014). At the same time, the Greek version of the neoliberal discourse accomodated the specificities of the domestic political and social environment, incorporating, "not necessarily fully or successfully", "the practices of statism, populism and clientelism, endemic in the Greek state (Featherstone 2011; Vasilopoulou et al. 2014)" (Doudaki et al. 2016, 441).

The coverage of the Greek crisis by international news media has been stereotypically fairly negative, naturalising the necessity of austerity policies (Arrese 2018; Mylonas 2012) without paying attention to the structural dimensions of the crisis (Tzogopoulos 2013; Bickes et al. 2014). The UK media, for example, in the early stages of the crisis, framed it "predominantly as a Greek problem that resulted from Greek economic policies with the Greek government and the people being held accountable" (Touri and Rogers 2013, 182). Also, US media, through narrow episodic frames that reproduced negative stereotypes about Greece, supported policies of severe austerity as a solution to the country's "alleged character flaws and ineptitudes" (Tracy 2012, 513). Similarly, in German media, the heavy employment of stereotypes about the "Greek character" (e.g. the irresponsible Greeks), fed by an Orientalist construction of Greeks as European "others", led to a culturalist–moralistic and even racist framing of the crisis as bearing cultural origins and being "self-inflicted" (Mylonas 2018, 140), while obscuring its systemic nature (Mylonas 2012, 2018). What is of importance for European politics is that "[t]he scandalization of the Greek crisis and the notion of crisis it 'catalysed' helped to forge a specific approach to crisis management and the reform of the European Economic and Monetary Union (EMU)" (Kutter 2014, 447). This was supported also by the risk-of-contagion discourse that was employed largely by international media, according to which the crisis in Greece was "conceptualized as a spreading disease that could affect the entire Eurozone" (Arrese and Vara-Miguel 2016, 145).

The role of elite actors, such as "self-interested politicians and financial markets' leaders", in these representations is crucial, as they have managed to supply "hostile framings" of Greece that have been adopted by international media (Kaitatzi-Whitlock 2014, 41). The dependence of media and journalists on elite institutional sources, such as government officials and business and economy experts (Mercille 2014; Tambini 2010) has extremely important repercussions for the news reporting of the economy and the financial crises (Berry 2012; Manning 2013; Thompson 2013). These sources are "overwhelmingly cited" in the news (Schiffrin and Fagan 2013, 151) and are given abundant opportunities to offer their versions of social reality (Rafter 2014), while alternative voices remain largely absent. Their dominant presence is related to the lack of "independence and critical judgment needed to investigate the financialisation of the economic system" (Schechter 2009, 20) and leads to high levels of co-orientation between journalists and their sources, in regard to the range of information, opinions, and interpretations of the crisis offered to the public (Knowles 2018; Doudaki et al. 2016, 2019). Reliance on elite sources is identified by Curran (2019, 191) as one of the three factors in the crisis of contemporary journalism, especially when journalists "say broadly the same thing, and when this accords with prevailing ideas that journalists themselves share". This dependence explains, for example, "why leading media in the US, Britain, Germany and Japan framed the possibility of the electoral victory of the far left Syriza party in Greece in 2012 as a threat to the international economy" (ibid.).

References

Ana.gr. 2017. "Defence Minister, ND's Georgiadis Trade Accusations in Parliament over Noor1 Drug Ship." 26 June. www.ana.gr/en/article/166419/.

Ana.gr. 2019. "Commissioner Vestager Expresses Support for Actions against Press Distribution Monopoly in Greece." 22 February. www.ana.gr/en/article/337140/.

Arrese, Ángel. 2018. "Austerity Policies in the European Press: A Divided Europe?" In *The Media and Austerity: Comparative Perspectives*, edited by Laura Basu, Steve Schifferes, and Sophie Knowles, 183–95. London: Routledge.

Arrese, Ángel, and Alfonso Vara-Miguel. 2016. "A Comparative Study of Metaphors in Press Reporting of the Euro Crisis." *Discourse & Society* 27 (2): 133–55.

Berger, Peter L., and Thomas Luckmann. 1967. *The Social Construction of Reality*. London: Penguin Books.

Berry, Mike. 2012. "The *Today* Programme and the Banking Crisis." *Journalism* 14 (2): 253–70.

Bickes, Hans, Tina Otten, and Laura Chelsea Weymann. 2014. "The Financial Crisis in the German and English Press: Metaphorical Structures in the Media Coverage on Greece, Spain and Italy." *Discourse & Society* 25 (4): 424–45.

Curran, James. 2019. "Triple Crisis of Journalism." *Journalism* 20 (1): 190–3.

Darzanou, Angela. 2013. "Αναζητούνται 'Συνολικές Λύσεις' για τις Ζημίες και τα Χρέη των ΜΜΕ." *I Avgi*, 28 December. http://avgi.gr/article/1574218/.

Doudaki, Vaia. 2015. "Legitimation Mechanisms in the Bailout Discourse." *Javnost: The Public* 22 (1): 1–17.

Doudaki, Vaia, Angeliki Boubouka, Lia-Paschalia Spyridou, and Christos Tzalavras. 2016. "Dependency, (Non)Liability and Austerity News Frames of Bailout Greece." *European Journal of Communication* 31 (4): 426–45.

Doudaki, Vaia, Angeliki Boubouka, and Christos Tzalavras. 2019. "Framing the Cypriot Financial Crisis: In the Service of the Neoliberal Vision." *Journalism* 20 (2): 349–68.

Ekathimerini.com. 2019. "Shipping Tycoon's Revelations Kick up Political Storm." 19 April. www.ekathimerini.com/239704/article/ekathimerini/news/shipping-tycoons-revelations-kick-up-political-storm.

Featherstone, Kevin. 2011. "The Greek Sovereign Debt Crisis and EMU: A Failing State in a Skewed Regime." *Journal of Common Market Studies* 49 (2): 193–217.

Hallin, Daniel C., and Paolo Mancini. 2004. *Comparing Media Systems: Three Models of Media and Politics*. Cambridge: Cambridge University Press.

Kaitatzi-Whitlock, Sophia. 2014. "The Eurozone Crisis and the Media: The Solution Is the Problem." *Javnost-The Public* 21 (4): 25–45.

Kapsalis, Apostolos. 2018. "Το Σύγχρονο Εργασιακό Τοπίο στα Μίντια [Current Working Landscape in the Media]." In special issue *100 Χρόνια Συνδικάτα [Trade Unions: 100 Years]*, 21–30. Journal of Institute of Employment GSEE, issue 244. www.inegsee.gr/wp-content/uploads/2018/12/NOEMBRIOS-DEKEMBRIOS-2018.pdf.

Keddie, Patrick. 2018. "Greek Game in Crisis and Nottingham Forest's Marinakis Is at the Heart of It." *The Observer*, 26 March. www.theguardian.com/football/2018/mar/26/greek-football-crisis-evangelos-marinakis-nottingham-forest-drug-trafficking-charges-olympiakos.

Knowles, Sophie. 2018. "Financial Journalists, the Financial Crisis and the 'Crisis' in Journalism." In *The Media and Austerity: Comparative Perspectives*, edited by Laura Basu, Steve Schifferes, and Sophie Knowles, 183–95. London: Routledge.

Kutter, Amelie. 2014. "A Catalytic Moment: The Greek Crisis in the German Financial Press." *Discourse & Society* 25 (4): 446–66.

Manning, Paul. 2013. "Financial Journalism, News Sources and the Banking Crisis." *Journalism* 14 (2): 173–89.

Mapping Media Freedom. 2019. "Greece." Map by the European Centre for Press & Media Freedom. Accessed 4 May 2019. https://mappingmediafreedom.org/index.php/country-profiles/greece/.

Mercille, Julien. 2014. "The Role of the Media in Sustaining Ireland's Housing Bubble." *New Political Economy* 19 (2): 282–301.

Ministry of Digital Policy, Telecommunications and Media. 2017. "Υπηρεσία Καταγραφής και Εντοπισμού Περιπτώσεων Λογοκλοπής στο Διαδίκτυο για τα Μέλη του Μητρώου Online Media." Press Release, 28 August. www.mindigital.gr/index.php/press-office-gr/%CE%B4%CE%B5%CE%BB%CF%84%CE%AF%CE%B1-%CF%84%CF%8D%CF%80%CE%BF%CF%85/1590-online-media.

Mylonas, Yiannis. 2012. "Media and the Economic Crisis of the EU: The 'Culturalization' of a Systemic Crisis and Bild-Zeitung's Framing of Greece." *tripleC* 10 (2): 646–71.

Mylonas, Yiannis. 2014. "Crisis, Austerity and Opposition in Mainstream Media Discourses of Greece." *Critical Discourse Studies* 11 (3): 305–21.

Mylonas, Yiannis. 2018. "Race and Class in German Media Representations of the 'Greek Crisis'." In *The Media and Austerity: Comparative Perspectives*, edited by Laura Basu, Steve Schifferes, and Sophie Knowles, 140–54. London: Routledge.

Naftemporiki.gr. 2017. "Shipowner Marinakis Submits Highest Bid for DOL Media Group." 31 May. www.naftemporiki.gr/story/1241709/.

Naftemporiki.gr. 2018. "Vocal Condemnation of Bomb Attack against Media Group; Issue of Skai 'Boycott' by Govt Re-Emerges." 17 December. www.naftemporiki.gr/story/1425295/.

News247.gr. 2014. "Τα Σκάνδαλα ΠΑΣΟΚ: Από το Καλαμπόκι στον Κοσκωτά και από το Χρηματιστήριο στον Τσοχατζόπουλο." 3 September. www.news247.gr/afieromata/ta-skandala-pasok-apo-to-kalampoki-ston-koskota-kai-apo-to-chrimatistirio-ston-tsochatzopoylo.6293439.html.

Papachristoudi, Matina. 2018. "Άγριος Εκδοτικός Πόλεμος χωρίς . . . Κοινό." *Mediatvnews.gr*, 5 December. http://mediatvnews.gr/?p=10156.

Papathanassopoulos, Stelios. 2004. *Πολιτική και ΜΜΕ. Η Περίπτωση της Νότιας Ευρώπης [Politics and Media: The Case of Southern Europe]*. Athens: Kastaniotis.

Papathanassopoulos, Stelios. 2015. "Απορρυθμίζοντας το Ελληνικό Επικοινωνιακό Σύστημα [Deregulating the Greek Broadcasting System]." In *Το Πολιτικό Πορτραίτο της Ελλάδας [The Political Portrait of Greece]*, edited by Nikos G. Georgarakis and Nicolas Demertzis, 456–75. Athens: Gutenberg Editions and National Centre for Social Research.

Papatheodorou, Fotini, and David Machin. 2003. "The Umbilical Cord That Was Never Cut: The Post-Dictatorial Intimacy between the Political Elite and the Mass Media in Greece and Spain." *European Journal of Communication* 18 (1): 31–54.

Pleios, George. 2015. "Οι Ειδήσεις της Κρίσης [The News of the Crisis]." In *Το Πολιτικό Πορτραίτο της Ελλάδας [The Political Portrait of Greece]*, edited by Nikos G. Georgarakis and Nicolas Demertzis, 494–520. Athens: Gutenberg Editions and National Centre for Social Research.

Psarras, Dimitris. 2016. *1922–2016 Συγκρότημα Λαμπράκη: Το βαθύ Κράτος του Τύπου [1922–1916 Lambrakis Group: The Deep State of the Press]. I Efimerida ton Syntakton*, 19 March, special edition.

Public Issue. 2018. "Εμπιστοσύνη στους Θεσμούς – Η ετήσια έρευνα της Public Issue για το 2018 [Trust in Institutions: The Annual Research of Public Issue for 2018]." 7 December. www.publicissue.gr/14830/institutions-2018/.

Rafter, Kevin. 2014. "Voices in the Crisis: The Role of Media Elites in Interpreting Ireland's Banking Collapse." *European Journal of Communication* 29 (5): 598–607.

Reporters without Borders. 2019. "2019 World Press Freedom Index: Greece." https://rsf.org/en/greece.

Schechter, Danny. 2009. "Credit Crisis: How Did We Miss It?" *British Journalism Review* 20 (1): 9–26.

Schiffrin, Anya, and Ryan Fagan. 2013. "Are We All Keynesians Now? The US Press and the American Recovery Act of 2009." *Journalism* 14 (2): 151–72.

Serafis, Dimitris, and Thierry Herman. 2018. "Media Discourse and Pathos: Sketching a Critical and Integrationist Approach: Greek and French Headlines before the Greek Referendum of 2015." *Social Semiotics* 28 (2): 184–200.

Siapera, Eugenia, Lambrini Papadopoulou, and Fragiskos Archontakis. 2015. "Post-Crisis Journalism." *Journalism Studies* 16 (3): 449–65.

Smyrnaios, Nikos. 2008. "Συγκέντρωση στα ΜΜΕ και Οικονομική Ολιγαρχία" [Media Concentration and Economic Oligarchy]. 7 May. http://ephemeron.eu/118.

Syllas, Christos. 2013. "Free Speech Takes a Beating in Greece." Index on Censorship, 25 March. www.indexoncensorship.org/2013/03/free-speech-takes-a-beating-in-greece/.

Tambini, Damian. 2010. "What Are Financial Journalists for?" *Journalism Studies* 11 (2): 158–74.

Thenationalherald.com, 2019. "Election Looming, Tsipras Ends SYRIZA Boycott of SKAI TV." 1 July. https://www.thenationalherald.com/251869/election-looming-tsipras-ends-syriza-boycott-of-skai-tv/.

Thompson, Peter A. 2013. "Invested Interests? Reflexivity, Representation and Reporting in Financial Markets." *Journalism* 14 (2): 208–27.

Touri, Maria, and Shani Lynn Rogers. 2013. "Europe's Communication Deficit and the UK Press: Framing the Greek Financial Crisis." *Journal of Contemporary European Studies* 21 (2): 175–89.

Tracy, James F. 2012. "Covering 'Financial Terrorism': The Greek Debt Crisis in US News Media." *Journalism Practice* 6 (4): 513–29.

Tzogopoulos, George. 2013. *The Greek Crisis in the Media: Stereotyping in the International Press*. London: Routledge.

Vasilopoulou, Sofia, Daphne Halikiopoulou, and Theofanis Exadaktylos. 2014. "Greece in Crisis: Austerity, Populism and the Politics of Blame." *JCMS: Journal of Common Market Studies* 52 (2): 388–402.

3 Discourses of legitimation in the news

Concepts and dimensions

Vaia Doudaki

Building journalistic authority through objectivity

Journalistic professionalism, at least as it has been developed by Anglo-American standards, is intrinsically tied to diverse sets of principles and practices constructed around objectivity. Objectivity is treated as the epitome of contemporary mainstream journalism, either as the unattainable – yet still necessary – ideal by which professional practice is evaluated, or as the framework that guides the everyday application of work methods.

The rise of the objectivity norm in the USA in the late 19th and early 20th centuries reflects, inter alia, the increased need and pursuit of journalists to build a distinct professional identity and achieve professional recognition[1] (Schudson 2001; Tuchman 1972). This would allow them to establish their authority in collecting and disseminating information in the form of news, and protect their territory from other professions.

According to sociologist Andrew Abbott (1988), the struggle for the recognition of a profession revolves around the struggle over jurisdiction. For Abbott, the professional field is a terrain of competition over jurisdiction in regard to what constitutes professional knowledge, which is broader than occupational knowledge, as it involves "a knowledge system governed by abstractions, a knowledge system that can redefine its problems and tasks, defend them from interlopers, and seize new problems" (93). Journalism's claim to objectivity represents the struggle over jurisdiction regarding the collection, evaluation, presentation, and distribution of information about current events. As Schudson and Anderson note,

> journalistic objectivity operates as *both* an occupational norm and as object of struggle within the larger struggle over professional jurisdiction. "Expert" professionals – in this case, journalists – seek, via occupational struggle, to monopolize a form of journalistic expertise, which

> itself is discursively constructed out of various journalistic practices and narratives, including the claim to professional objectivity.
>
> (2009, 96, emphasis in original)

Within this vein, the construction of the objectivity norm is related to the struggle to build an epistemology of journalism that will allow for the recognition of journalism as a profession and a disciplinary field. Even from the early days, American journalist and author Walter Lippmann (1920) argued for the need to develop an episteme, which was considered crucial to the establishment of journalism as a profession: "There is but one kind of unity possible in a world as diverse as ours. It is unity of method, rather than of aim; the unity of the disciplined experiment" (67), "in which the ideal of objective testimony is cardinal" (82). Building an episteme that comprises "the unity of the disciplined experiment" has been a rather challenging endeavour, even more so since journalism is neither a scientific nor an academic discipline. For example, during the early period of journalism's development and establishment as a recognised profession, it had to fight with professions like public relations for jurisdiction over the collection and presentation of information in the form of news (Schudson 1978, 2001, 163). Journalism's recognition as both a profession and a disciplinary field has been crucial to its acknowledgement as one of the main societal institutions of authority, that of the "fourth estate" (safeguarding democracy through its vigilant scrutiny of the "other three estates" – the legislative, the executive and the judicial) (Schultz 1998; McQuail 2013, 39–41).

Reflecting on the nature and dimensions of objectivity, Ward (2010, 139) argued that "news objectivity, with its stress on facts, empirical methods, and impartial procedures" combines the ontological, epistemological and procedural senses of objectivity. Adding one important dimension, Schudson (2001, 149) maintained that "'[o]bjectivity' is at once a moral ideal, a set of reporting and editing practices, and an observable pattern of news writing". Examining this "observable pattern of news writing", Figdor described as objective the news reports "that can provide testimonial knowledge or justified belief about some aspect of the world to those who read or hear them" (2010, 153). One way or another, these approaches and definitions point to the fact that objectivity is both a theoretical and a practical endeavour, a long-term orientation and commitment, and an everyday micro practice.

Since objectivity is not only a method, a set of principles, tools and practices guiding news production, but also the output of this work method, over the years a set of news-writing conventions have been developed, in regard to what constitutes an "objective news story". These conventions, reflecting the doctrine of objectivity, are built around the standards of factuality, truthfulness, impartiality, balance, fairness, and neutrality (McQuail 1992;

Westerståhl 1983; Ward 2010, 142; Schudson 2001, 150). They concern both news gathering and news writing, and can be traced in the news stories themselves. Based on these standards, journalists should present fact-based and verifiable accounts of events, which are as complete as possible and as accurate as possible, not omitting any important piece of information, presenting the different sides of an issue in a non-biased way, with journalists not taking sides. Also, "objective" journalists should separate facts from opinion, minimising their own "presence" in the story.

GayeTuchman (1972) identified a set of "strategic procedures, exemplified as the formal attributes of a news story" (665), which enable journalists to claim objectivity and which relate to the standards just discussed. These procedures focus on the presentation of "conflicting possibilities related to truth-claims", in the news stories, which supports the standards of balance and fairness; the presentation of supplementary evidence to support facts, which is related to factuality and truthfulness; the use of quotation marks to indicate that journalists take some distance from their sources' truth claims, which serves the standards of impartiality and neutrality; the structuring of information in an "appropriate sequence" by prioritising what is supposed to be the most important information concerning an event, which supports the preponderance of factuality in objective news reporting; and, finally, the separation of facts from opinions, which is related to neutrality and impartiality (676).

Among the standards of objectivity, factuality stands out as an overarching principle, being supported and served by all the other constituents of objectivity. Affirmations often used by journalists such as "facts are sacred"[2] or "facts speak for themselves" illustrate the embeddedness of the ethos of factuality in journalistic practice. News, in everyday practice, involves a continuous processing and repackaging of occurrences as facts. Through the commitment to reporting those occurrences of social life identified as facts, journalists are bestowed with the authority of an almost scientific method of work, especially since what is presented by journalists as fact is endowed with the quality of verifiability. As Tuchman argues, "the assertion that 'the facts speak for themselves' [. . .] implies an everyday distinction between the 'speaking facts' and the reporter (speechmaker, gossiper, etc.) speaking for the 'facts'" (1972, 667). This distinction helps to construct a distance between the journalist and the facts s/he is delivering to the audience, thus attesting to the model of the journalist as an organic (in the Gramscian sense; see Gramcsi 1971, 10) social scientist.

Also, the practice of interviewing, which became popular in the early 20th century in the USA (and later in Europe), is part of the effort to construct an objective fact-based episteme. The related practice of systematically using quotes from news sources that are collected through interviews, public statements, etc. serves as a proof of the journalists collecting information through sources, not being dependent on their own senses while reporting the news (Schudson 1982, 1995, 2001, 156). This also facilitates the separation of fact from opinion, as opinion is left to the journalists' quoted sources. According to Tuchman (1972, 668), the use of quotations helps "to remove the reporter's presence from the story", even if in practice quotations are often used surreptitiously to convey the journalist's and the news organisation's opinion on the topic, attributing it to their quoted sources.

This "testimonial knowledge" (Figdor 2010, 153) and "observable pattern of newswriting" (Schudson 2001, 149) are related to the construction of not only the ethics and practice of objectivity, but also of its form and aesthetics, which brings us to the logics – and ideal – of the objective narrative.

The ideal of the objective narrative

News is a product of the inherent tension that stems from the need to present news as facts through a story format. News is expected to be based on facts; however, it cannot be reduced to facts only – as it cannot be reduced to (fictional) stories. In practice, news consists of events narrated as stories with a beginning, a middle, and an end, which contain a synthesis of "clear" and "incontestable" facts. In order to deliver this kind of news, journalists – driven by the axiom of objectivity – fragment the messy social reality and reconstruct it as facts, which are then narrated as stories.

However, stories should not only be written objectively (as regards method and process) but also "emit" objectivity in that they bear the proof of objectivity in ways that can be easily recognised by employers, peers, and the public. To deal with these challenges, journalists have developed a number of formal and stylistic conventions to guarantee that the outcome of the processes that put into practice the ideals and norms of objectivity is "evidently" objective and produces an objective journalistic narrative. These conventions are, among others, the inverted pyramid model, the use of (quoted) sources in the news text, the inclusion of "both sides" of the story, and the separation of facts from opinion.

Still, even if these conventions attempt to construct objectivity as form and as style and to tackle the inherent contradiction in the "objective story" claim, they give ground to other contradictions. For example, studying the emergence of American journalism in 19th and 20th centuries, Schudson (1982, 1995) described how news writing moved from providing chronological accounts of events to employing other conventions, such as the summary lead and the inverted pyramid structure. While this shift is related, inter alia, to the pursue of an objectivity-led professionalism, it actually prompted journalists to move away from being stenographers to being interpreters (Schudson 1982, 102, 1995, 59). Another example comes from the convention of separation of facts from opinion: It is not uncommon for the opinion of different actors that appear in the news to be treated as fact – and the higher the authority position of the involved actors, the higher the frequency of treating the opinions of these actors as facts.

The journalistic narrative conventions used as a testimony of journalists' attachment to the norms of objectivity also serve to consolidate the journalists' position as an "authoritative interpretive community" (Zelizer 1992). "While all professional groups are constituted by formalized bodies of knowledge, much of journalists' professional authority lies not in what they know, but in how they represent their knowledge", argues Zelizer (ibid., 34), who maintains that the use of narrative in strategic ways helps journalists "to establish themselves as authoritative spokespersons" (ibid., 32). According to Buozis and Creech (2018, 1436), "news narratives exist as both the products of standardized journalistic routines and evidence of broader cultural forces at play, cultural forces that rely upon journalism's implicit authority over the truth". As Zelizer (2004, 103) further explains, journalists' claims of authority over the truth are inextricably tied to the legitimation of their professional authority:

> Journalism's presumed legitimacy depends on its declared ability to provide an indexical and referential presentation of the world at hand. Insisting on the centrality of reality, and on facts as its carrier, for maintaining a clear distinction between itself and other domains of public discourse, journalists claim a capacity to narrativize the events in the real world that distinguishes them from other cultural voices, retaining an attentiveness to how things "really" happened as the premise by which journalism makes its name.

Hence, the journalistic narrative is constructed by, but also constructs, the norm of objectivity, while journalistic authority is performed through rituals, conventions, and practices that engage with objectivity and reaffirm journalism as a privileged knowledge field.

News sources, objectivity, and authority building

The journalistic paradigm of a scientific-like method of work is supported by the process of news gathering, "where reporters gather authoritative data and then present it without explicitly taking a side in the discourse" (Berkowitz 2009, 103). By following this process, journalists "become society's scientists and the news they produce becomes their 'scientific report' – their truth" (ibid.). As previously mentioned, the clear, unquestionable presence of sources in the news stories – through the practice of interviewing and using direct, quoted speech – is used as a testimony of journalists' objective methods that serves the construction and reconstruction of journalistic authority.

Highlighting the importance of sources, Sigal (1986, 29) asserted: "News is, after all, not what journalists think, but what their sources say, and is mediated by news organizations, journalistic routines and conventions, which screen out many of the personal predilections of individual journalists". Of course, one could argue that it is the journalists' personal and organisational "predilections" that drive the selection of news sources in the first place. Journalists' reliance on sources to provide them (information about) the facts, apart from a token of objectivity, is also a protective mechanism since "sources and not journalists are responsible for the accuracy of the facts" (Soloski 1989, 214). This helps to shield journalists and their news organisations from charges of bias and inaccurate reporting (Tuchman 1972, 668–9).

Of course, the qualification of an actor or institution as a source is neither natural nor straightforward. As numerous scholars have pointed out, news is dominated by a very narrow range of actors who are treated as its privileged sources, and who represent mainly political, economic, and other institutional elites (Reese 1990; Iyengar 1994; Gitlin 1980) resulting in "a systematically structured over-accessing to the media of those in powerful and privileged institutional positions" (Hall et al. 1978, 58). These actors are given the opportunity by the media to act not only as information carriers, but also as primary definers of events (ibid.) and as "sponsors of the frames" (Carragee and Roefs 2004, 219) within which the events of social, political, and economic life will be reconstructed and interpreted. This dependence of journalists and news media on elite institutional sources and the largely uncritical adoption of their preferred interpretations results in an "institutional bias" on reality, since "together with the information the worldview of these elites is also adopted and presented as the orthodox perception over social reality" (Doudaki 2015, 10). Through this process of institutionalisation, these elite actors "are objectified as the legitimate and legitimating sources of both information and governance" (Tuchman 1978, 210).

This attachment to a narrow vision of what or who qualifies as a news source is connected to the attachment to a restricted vision of objectivity. When reporting on the news, journalists who adhere to a narrow notion of objectivity tend to treat the current politico-economic system as given by the natural order, and they over rely on institutional sources who represent the power structure of society: "By perpetuating as commonsensical notions of who ought to be treated as authoritative" through the acceptance of frames imposed on events by officials and the marginalisation of "voices that fall outside the dominant elite circles", "these routines help the system maintain control without sacrificing legitimacy" (Reese 1990, 425). As Berkowitz argues (2009, 106), "when the interface between reporters and their sources produces and reproduces a specific frame, a specific vantage point on the social order is propagated and maintained". Put slightly differently, Soloski (1989, 225) maintains that "news professionalism biases news at a societal level", given that "the professional norms legitimize the existing order by making it appear to be a naturally occurring state of affairs".

Through their privileged presence in the news, elite sources gain a designated space from which to not only support their positions (and discredit those of opponents), but also to claim and legitimate their authority (and delegitimise the authority position of other actors). In practice, the presence of elite sources in the news serves multiple functions of legitimation and authority building. As already mentioned, through their authoritative presence, they (de)legitimate not only policies and actions, but also authority positions. At the same time, elite sources help journalists to maintain their professional authority, through confirmation of the dominant model of objective journalism. Media and institutional sources engage in processes of inter- and intra-legitimation and authority building: Elite sources are given a privileged position in the news and their views are hardly ever challenged, being in most occasions implicitly or explicitly supported by journalists; institutional sources, for their part, acknowledge and give value to journalists' right to act as the institutional communicators and mediators of the major societal and political issues (preferably echoing the sources' versions and interpretations of these issues). Hence, journalists and their sources enhance each other's status, legitimacy, and power, in a process of mutual authority confirmation and enhancement.[3]

The processes and practices of mutual legitimation between journalists and their sources bear significant implications for the authority of journalists and the news they produce, which brings us to the broader issue of the ideological function of news.

News and ideology

The journalistic practices of news gathering and news writing, and thus the conventions and qualities of news storytelling, have ideological ramifications at the levels of journalistic professionalism, journalistic authority, and journalistic output. Critical and cultural studies scholars, building on the seminal work on power and ideology of Gramsci (1971, 1999) and Althusser (1971), have paid considerable attention to the ways in which these practices help to establish societal consent around particular ideologies, which acquire hegemonic status, treated as common-sense and given by the natural order (Hall 1979; Hall et al. 1978; Gitlin 1980; Williams 1977). These scholars focus on ideology from a range of perspectives, examining the ways in which "symbolic forms" and news, in particular, "intersect with relations of power" and "the ways in which meaning is mobilized in the social world and served thereby to bolster up individuals and groups who occupy positions of power" (Thompson 1990, 56).

Studies on ideology have attributed particular significance to the role and function of hegemony. Gramsci (1971) was the first to broaden the scope of hegemony, not limiting it to class power and to the political and economic dominance of a certain group over others, but encompassing the dimension of cultural dominance (Bates 1975; Scott 2001, 89). For Gramsci, hegemony "entails moral, political, and intellectual leadership within a social system" (Reese 1990, 394). Along these lines, consent becomes a core apparatus of hegemony and source of power for the hegemonic groups. A dominant ideology is not imposed on subordinate groups by force;[4] rather, through its diffusion through culture and the major societal institutions – the media being one of them – it is reproduced, acknowledged, and widely accepted, even by social groups whose interests are not supported by it (Dow 1990, 262; Scott 2001, 89). For Gitlin (1980, 253), hegemony is the "systematic (but not necessarily or even usually deliberate) engineering of mass consent to the established order". It this way, "the ruling group does not simply impose a class ideology on others but rather provides the articulating principle by which diverse ideological elements are unified into a world-view" (Reese 1990, 394). Hence, hegemony is performed in

> the myriad of everyday institutional activities and experiences that culminate in "common sense," thus hiding the choices made and "mystifying" the interests of dominant groups. Dominant group definitions of reality, norms, and standards appear as normal rather than as political and contestable.
>
> (Deetz 1977, 62)

Concealing the constructed nature of systems of beliefs and the contingency of the social is a genuinely ideological function. As Willis argues, "[o]ne of the most important general functions of ideology is the way in which it turns uncertain and fragile cultural resolutions and outcomes into a pervasive naturalism" (1977, 162). It is actually in "pervasive naturalism" where the common-sense power of ideology lies: "[W]hen ideology becomes common sense, it apparently ceases to be ideology; this is itself an ideological effect, for ideology is truly effective only when it is disguised" (Fairclough 2015, 126).

The media, and news in particular, have been a privileged terrain for the naturalisation and concealment of ideology. As previously mentioned, news is a product of the inherent tension stemming from its dual nature (news as facts and as stories). Both the factual and the narrative logic of news, and the practices that serve them, are value-laden. It has already been discussed how the axiom of objectivity supports news gathering and news writing practices and output that stay close to the hegemonic discourses of society. Still, the ideological implications of the narrative logic of news deserve some more attention.

As information needs to be conveyed in frameworks that are meaningful for the audience, journalists often resort to easily identifiable symbolic means and structures, drawn from culture, the historic past, etc., for the presentation of their stories (Van Gorp 2007, 2010). Narratives serve thus "the important function of educating an audience by portraying what constitutes a legitimate and/or an illegitimate practice" by highlighting "certain aspects of an event while neglecting or diminishing others so that the moral can be readily apprehended" (Reshef and Keim 2014, 152). These discursive schemata bring with them ethical, aesthetic, and other sets of values, together with the ideological burden that those carry. These meaningful frameworks cannot be ideology-free, as they entail assumptions about what social reality means and how society should be organised. As Bird and Dardenne (1988, 71) argue, "[n]ews stories, like myths, do not 'tell it like it is,' but rather, 'tell it like it means'", and any suggestion of a certain meaning goes hand in hand with a set of (ideological) values.

Hence, narratives are seen to contribute to the formation and maintenance of value systems, operating as the shells that carry and protect society's main cultural and ideological conventions. Along these lines, news stories function as particularly

> compelling and persuasive discursive forms through which our values, norms, and political preferences are cultivated and reinforced; over time, the "unity," coherence and moral certainty that they supply offer us the seductive prospect of anchoring ourselves within a particular view of the world.
>
> (Gunster and Saurette 2014, 337)

As Schudson notes, "[i]t is a very different matter to say the news reflects the social world by describing it, and to say that it reflects the social world by incorporating it into unquestioned and unnoticed conventions of narration" (1982, 106). These opaque conventions of narration create the conditions for news to "circulate as cultural artifacts bearing truthful representations that make sense within the broader relations of power" (Buozis and Creech 2018, 1433).

Within this logic, news narratives can "serve to justify the exercise of power by those who possess it and [. . .] to reconcile others to the fact that they do not" (Thompson 1990, 62). They

> portray social relations and unfold the consequences of action, in ways that may establish and sustain relations of power [. . .] [by] recounting the way that the world appears and [. . .] reinforcing [. . .] the apparent order of things.
>
> (ibid.)

News is a privileged terrain for such confirmations, even more so than other cultural products, as it supposedly provides factual and accurate accounts of the events that constitute social reality. "[T]hrough its support of hegemonic structures and through the continued proliferation of news' story forms as commonsense ways of representing the world" (Buozis and Creech 2018, 1434), the seemingly neutral style of journalism is inherently ideological. In practice, news not only reflects but also contributes to "the workings of ideology and the broader relations of power in society, relations often predicated upon journalism's seemingly stable representation of truth" (ibid., 1432).

Authority and legitimation in times of crisis

For (hegemonic) ideologies to secure consent, they and their related actors and institutions need to be acknowledged as legitimate. Also, the carriers of these ideologies need to be recognised as having the necessary authority to act as their communicators and enact these ideologies.

Authority can be understood as the recognised or delegated power to accomplish a task, or as the right to exercise some form of power, which is usually socially endorsed or justified (Spady and Mitchell 1979, 101). Thompson (1990, 59) sees authority as "a socially or institutionally endowed capacity which enables or empowers some individuals to make decisions, pursue ends or realize interests". According to Torfing (1999, 165), authority is "an exercise of power that is accepted by those who are subjected to it". Also, Lindblom (1977, 17–8) argues that authority exists "whenever one, several, or many people explicitly or tacitly permit someone else to make decisions for them for some category of acts". Central in these definitions is the permission granted to the authority-holders, since this authority is not exerted by the use of force or violence. Additionally, the actors who act as "organic intellectuals" (Gramsci 1971, 10) (e.g., journalists, experts, teachers, scientists), and their related institutions (media, education, church, etc.) that ground the conditions of voluntary acceptance or permission, play a crucial role in the naturalisation of authority. These actors and institutions create the conditions for the "sources of authority" (Torfing 1999, 167) to function "as the privileged reference points for the authorization of power" presenting them as natural and always there, and not as "constructed in and through political power struggles" (ibid.).

Authority building functions in a reciprocal fashion with multiplying effects: The action, narrative, policy, office or institution that is legitimated as authoritative helps the involved actors to build their own authority, and vice versa. It may be that "[t]he power of any narrative to suggest what should be is dependent upon the authority of its narrator" (Baym 2000, 95), but at the same time the authoritative power of narratives helps the narrators to build their authority through association with them: "If successful, legitimation [of authority] not only implies the endorsement of specific actions, but usually also extends to the dominant group or institutions themselves, as well as to their position and leadership" (Rojo and Van Dijk 1997, 528).

Max Weber (2015) identified three main types of (political) authority: traditional authority, which is legitimated through tradition and custom; rational-legal authority, legitimated through laws and bureaucracy; and charismatic authority, legitimated through morality, truthfulness, and personal charisma. The institutional actors that appear in the news try to relate to all three types of authority. The clearer their connection to one – or preferably more than one – type of authority is, and the narratives that support them, the easier it can be for them to be identified as actors of authority. Similarly, the clearer their connection to the institutions affiliated to these types of authority is, the easier it can be for them to be recognised as the authoritative spokespersons of these institutions. These processes help these actors to not only be "in authority" but also to be recognised as authorities themselves[5] (Buzzelli and Johnston 2001, 874).

Critical in the recognition of authority is its legitimation. According to Weber (1978, 213), every system of authority "attempts to establish and to cultivate the belief in its legitimacy", seeking "normative approval for its policies or actions" (Rojo and Van Dijk 1997, 528). Berger and Luckmann argue that legitimation is the process of "explaining and justifying" the institutional order, by "ascribing cognitive validity to its objectivated meanings" and "giving a normative dignity to its practical imperatives" (1967, 111). According to the authors, legitimation functions as a "'second-order' objectivation of meaning" making "objectively available and subjectively plausible the 'first-order' objectivations that have been institutionalized" (1967, 110). It thus "not only tells the individual why he *should* perform one action and not another; it also tells him why things *are* what they are" (ibid., 111, emphasis in original).

Put more broadly, legitimation involves the processes and practices of establishing "a generalized perception or assumption that the actions of an entity are desirable, proper, or appropriate within some socially constructed system of norms, values, beliefs, and definitions" (Suchman 1995, 574; see also Richardson 1985; Dowling and Pfeffer 1975). This approach to legitimation raises two important issues. First, it points to the fact that, for legitimation attempts to be successful, they should be "desirable to an audience and congruent with its definitions of right and wrong, acceptable and unacceptable, proper and improper" (Reshef and Keim 2014, 12–3). Second, since legitimation relates to the "creation of a sense of positive, beneficial, ethical, understandable, necessary or otherwise acceptable action in a specific setting" (Vaara 2014, 503), what rises as important is context: Legitimation is context-sensitive (Van Leeuwen 2007, 92); it is not guaranteed that the action or discourse that is recognised as legitimate in one occasion or setting will be treated as legitimate later in time or in other social, political, and cultural environments.

Within this frame, legitimation strategies concern the ways in which the actors of the different systems of authority (members of the political, economic or cultural elites) "mobilize discursive resources to impart a sense of legitimacy to their own actions and arguments while casting a long shadow on those of their opponents" (Reshef and Keim 2014, 18). The news media act as one of the main fields where the elite actors employ discursive strategies of legitimation, aiming to show that their actions and policies "are consistent with the *moral order* of society, that is, within the system of laws, norms, agreements or aims agreed upon by (the majority of) the citizens" (Rojo and Van Dijk 1997, 528, emphasis in original). Through their presence in the news, these actors have the opportunity to work on the legitimation of their own positions and roles (ibid., 550) by: (a) attempting to transfer the authority and legitimacy of the institution they represent, to them, monopolising social legitimacy; (b) "presenting discourse as a reflection of reality [. . .] by a process of objectivation", attempting thus to monopolise the truth; and (c) attempting to monopolise discourse, presenting themselves as the (only) "legitimate forces and legitimate social groups [that] have a right to an authorized discourse".

The struggle, and the need, to legitimate actions, policies, and (authority) positions become stronger in times of crisis – in this case economic crisis – given that the series of decisions and measures taken to tackle it have usually major social repercussions. As already mentioned, in the case of the economic crisis in Greece, the bailout agreements and the measures taken for their implementation followed, to a large extent, a neoliberal logic, prioritisng, above all, the protection of the banking system and sees the safeguarding of the welfare state as an obstacle to capitalist expansion (Harvey 2005). The terms of the agreements and the implemented measures of extreme austerity were, and still are, painful for Greek society – and some of these were highly contested and critiqued by both domestic and international actors and scholars as inefficient and unnecessarily harsh (see, e.g. Hall 2018; Pagoulatos 2018).

Also, political parties from almost the entire political spectrum in Greece have been part of governments that were involved in the negotiations, agreements, and implementation of these agreements. These conditions created a legitimation crisis for different groups and at different levels: The left and socialist parties that had been in government were found to implement neoliberal policies at odds with their proclaimed main ideological positions; also, the elected Greek governments seemed to have lost the authority of executive power, being forced to succumb to, or willingly accepting Troika's power; in addition, a number of measures that were voted by the Greek parliament were considered as falling within a shady area of (un)constitutionality (Papavlassopoulos 2015, 157–8). Therefore, the need to legitimate the implemented policies and measures, and the role of the involved actors, has been vital.

As the severe contestation and fierce political conflicts that these policies involve, but also the obligation to abide by harsh terms imposed by supra powers and institutions of authority (in this case, the Troika) damage the authority positions of the involved – mostly domestic – actors, the latter attempt to develop repair strategies in order to maintain and (re)establish their authority positions. For this purpose, they need, and are given, access to platforms of legitimation, such as the legacy news outlets. Of course, these conditions also create opportunities for other groups and actors to claim or (re)establish their authority as the privileged truth-holders of the crisis and its handling. For example, after getting 4.6% of the vote in the 2009 elections,[6] the left-wing Syriza managed to win the 2015 elections and come into power on an anti-Memorandum and anti-austerity agenda.

The Greek (elite) media themselves have been suffering from a major crisis, which goes beyond their financial viability and survival. Their remit as an institution that is independently reporting on the economic crisis has been seriously questioned on several occasions in which they failed to report accurately on the crisis. One major example of such a "failure" is their prediction that the result of the July 2015 referendum on the Troika's bailout proposal would be "yes" (Hiotis 2015; Tziovaras 2015), while it was massively rejected by the Greek electorate.

This study focusses on the analysis of news texts related to the economic crisis in Greece, and the journalistic practices that relate to their production, in order to identify the struggles over legitimation and authority building, since news acts as a privileged field for their articulation and mediation. As Carpentier and De Cleen argue (2007, 274),

> media are seen not just as passively expressing or reflecting social phenomena, but as specific machineries that produce, reproduce and transform social phenomena. The media are not just one of the societal sites where discourses circulate, but also discursive machineries that can be considered – using Foucault's (1972: 37–8) concept – "systems of dispersion" of discourses, with their proper and specific rules of formation.

As it will become clear later on in the analysis, journalists and news media have an active role in legitimating the policies, decisions, and measures that are related to the economic crisis, as well as in helping the dominant actors to establish and legitimate their authority (which in turn helps the journalists to legitimate their own role and authority). However, it should be acknowledged that since discursive practices are not performed in a social vacuum, one needs to also take into consideration the environment of discursive practices and its relation to social practices, which highlights the study's affinity with critical discourse analysis (CDA).

Studying news discourse with critical discourse analysis

This treatise uses the analytical toolbox of CDA. This theoretically informed methodological and analytical compass is considered suitable for the purposes of the study, given its focus on examining "*both* the discursive practices which construct representations of the world, social subjects and social relations, including power relations, *and* the role that these discursive practices play in furthering the interests of particular social groups" (Jørgensen and Phillips 2002, 63; emphasis in original).

Discourse, according to Norman Fairclough, is "language as a form of social practice determined by social structures" (2015, 51). It "is language" but "not just language". It is "'semiosis' [. . .] meaning-making and the resources that are used in it" (ibid., 8). Discourse "both reproduces and changes knowledge, identities and social relations including power relations, and at the same time is also shaped by other social practices and structures" (Jørgensen and Phillips 2002, 65), being thus "a stake in social struggle as well as a site of social struggle" (Fairclough 2015, 3).

This study adopts a meso-macro textual and contextual approach to discourse. It sees "texts as materializations of meaning and/or ideology" (Carpentier and De Cleen 2007, 277), focussing on the meanings and ideologies embedded in the texts and less on the language used (which is still examined to the degree that it is indicative of the meaning produced). Also, "whilst in micro-contextual approaches the context remains confined to specific social settings (such as a conversation), macro-contextual approaches refer to the social as the realm where the processes of the generation of meaning are situated" (ibid.). Although our analysis is not confined to a specific setting, it does examine the specificities of the texts and of journalistic practice, relating them to the social realm.

Fairclough identifies three dimensions that need to be studied in order to understand how discourse is produced: text, discursive practice, and social practice (1992, 62–100). In Fairclough's three-dimensional conception of discourse, which is anchored in the position that "social structures not only determine discourse, they are also a product of discourse" (2015, 68), texts shape and are shaped by social practice through discursive practice.

Operationalising this model into a methodological guide, Fairclough argues that the textual dimension of analysis should focus not only on a text's formal features (e.g. vocabulary, grammar, cohesion, text structure, etc.), but also on its meaning. The dimension of discursive practice relates to the processes of text production, distribution, and consumption. This dimension focusses analytically on the specificity of ways and of social contexts in which texts are produced, distributed, consumed, and interpreted. According to Fairclough, the analysis of discursive practice should involve a combination of "micro-analysis" and "macro-analysis" (1992, 85), that is, an examination of the ways in which "participants produce and interpret texts on the basis of their members' resources" combined with a macro-analysis of "the nature of the members' resources [. . .] that is being drawn upon in order to produce and interpret texts" (ibid.).

Examining discourse as social practice, Fairclough focusses on ideology and hegemonic power, investigating whether discursive practices performed in specific social contexts help in the reproduction or questioning of power relations. For Fairclough, ideologies are "significations/constructions of reality (the physical world, social relations, social identities), which are built into various dimensions of the forms/meanings of discursive practices" (1992, 87), and "which can be shown to contribute to establishing, maintaining and changing social relations of power, domination and exploitation" (2003, 9). In the same vein, hegemony is seen as "leadership as much as domination across the economic, political, cultural and ideological domains of a society" (1992, 92). At the same time, Fairclough acknowledges the contingent nature of the social, in line with discourse theory scholars Ernesto Laclau and Chantal Mouffe (1985), arguing that hegemony "is never achieved more than partially and temporarily, as an 'unstable equilibrium'" (Fairclough 1992, 92). Within this framework, the concept of hegemony is a useful tool to analyse "the social practice within which the discourse belongs in terms of power relations, in terms of whether they reproduce, restructure or challenge existing hegemonies" but also "discourse practice itself as a mode of hegemonic struggle, reproducing, restructuring or challenging existing orders of discourse" (ibid., 95).

When it comes to investigating the news coverage of the economic crisis in Greece, while focussing on the systematic examination of news texts, one needs to take also into consideration the journalistic practice that relates to the conventions of news production – including the news-gathering practices and the relations of journalists with their sources (as well as the conditions of news consumption, which is beyond the scope of this study), and also how news relates to social practice. To address the importance of journalistic practice, which, in our study includes conventions of journalistic culture and practices of news production, we employ an adjusted version of Fairclough's model. While Fairclough's model distinguishes text, discursive practice and social practice as the three analytical dimensions of discourse, the three interrelated dimensions of our model are news texts, journalistic practice and social practice (Figure 3.1). Compared to Fairclough's model, journalistic practice is located between discursive practice and social practice (being broader than discursive practice and narrower than social practice). Journalistic practice involves the journalists' relations and interactions with other journalists, with diverse types of actors (e.g., news sources), with the

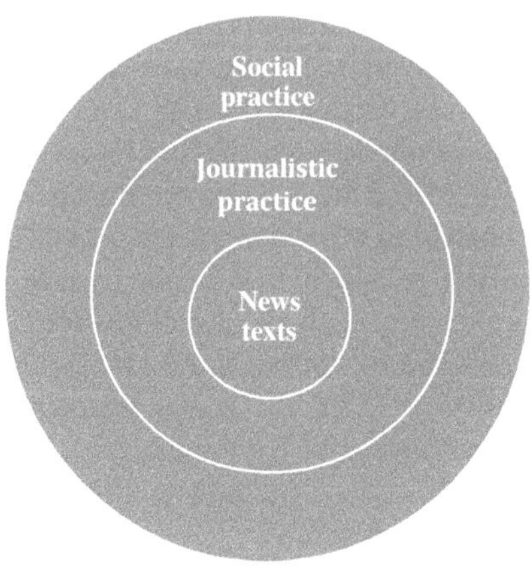

Figure 3.1 Studying discourse: levels of analysis

organisation they work for, and with their social environment; it includes multiple sources of influence; it involves professional and social norms, cultural practices, and their performance; it also involves power relations, processes of negotiation of meaning, and negotiation of identities and power positions of all the involved actors. Social practice, in this study, relates to the degree to which these journalistic practices and the news produced through these practices contribute to the cementation or destabilisation of the hegemonic discourse about the economic crisis, and of the authority positions and power configurations of the actors involved – including the journalists.

This study does not claim that all components and dimensions of journalistic and social practice have been investigated exhaustively. Still, the elements and dimensions of journalistic and social practice that are directly related to the cases and issues examined are incorporated in the analysis. It should also be made clear that the three levels of analysis are intertwined; the distinction of three different analytical spheres is to a degree artificial and serves the systematic examination of news discourse as practice, influenced by and influencing journalistic practice, and the broader social practice. For this purpose, embedding the journalistic output (i.e., the news texts) that is being examined into its socio-political environment is considered pertinent to the analysis, as it sheds light and helps to evaluate and interpret the produced discourses and the power struggles taking place each time.

Identifying discourses of legitimation

This chapter started by discussing major issues in, and dimensions of, journalistic practice that relate to professionalisation and the implementation of values and norms, driven by the axion of objectivity. It also addressed the special role of news sources in these practices and dealt with the factual/narrative logic of news, as well as the processes and practices developed by journalists to deal with the tension stemming from this dual logic. It then addressed the ideological implications of these journalistic practices for the produced news, and discussed the features and dimensions of authority and legitimation, in the context of the economic crisis in Greece. Finally, it presented CDA as a suitable analytical tool for the purposes of this study. The reason behind the systematic analysis of legitimation and its mechanisms is that it makes it possible to scrutinise the ideological implications and dimensions of journalistic practice, as it is crystallised in the produced news. In this section, the mechanisms of legitimation will be discussed in some detail, including how they operate and how to identify them in the journalistic texts and in journalistic practice.

News is not a neutral product of automated professional routines; it is produced by the interplay of social, political, economic, and cultural forces distilled into professional principles and practices. Hence, every news text, even the shortest news report, includes a lot of legitimising information on the reasons why it is presented and should be treated as news. Thus, an examination of the legitimising practices allows the unpacking of the assumptions, preferences, and ideological biases behind the set of choices of inclusion, exclusion, prioritisation, and their accompanying value judgements around the construction of news. Focussing specifically on news sources makes it possible to investigate the complex processes of inter- and intra-legitimation as well as authority confirmation between journalists and their sources. One other level of legitimation, as already discussed, concerns the hegemonic discourses of major societal issues – in our case the economic crisis and its handling – that circulate through the news media, which functions as a privileged space for orchestrating consent (but also for counter-discourses to circulate and gain legitimacy).

In order to identify legitimation discourse in the news, a conceptual and analytical model has been developed that identifies two overarching legitimation discourses – objectivation and naturalisation – which relate to the factual/narrative logic of news (see Figure 3.2). As will be elaborated later on, objectivation comprises expertise, quantification, and reification, while naturalisation consists of symbolic annihilation (omission, trivialisation, condemnation), mystification, and moralisation (see Table 3.1). The study explores how objectivation and naturalisation help to legitimate policies and positions of authority, via the use of sources in the news texts studied and their related journalistic practices.

An initial version of this framework that focussed explicitly on news texts and not on journalistic practice was developed in 2015 to examine the news coverage of the economic crisis in Greece (Doudaki 2015). This framework was updated in 2018 for an examination of the news coverage of the economic crisis in Cyprus (Doudaki 2018), and was further updated, enriched, and adjusted for the purposes of this study.

The framework profits from the work of Van Leeuwen and Wodak on legitimation discourse (Van Leeuwen 2007; Van Leeuwen and Wodak 1999), as well as from Thompson's (1990) work on ideology, bearing at the same time significant differences from the models developed by these

Table 3.1 Discourses of legitimation

Objectivation	*Naturalisation*
Expertise	Symbolic annihilation (omission, trivialisation, condemnation)
Quantification	Mystification
Reification	Moralisation

scholars. The model developed by Van Leeuwen and Wodak (Van Leeuwen 2007; Van Leeuwen and Wodak 1999) – which a number of scholars have used in its original or a modified version for analyses on legitimation discourse – identifies four main categories of legitimation: authorisation, moral evaluation, rationalisation, and mythopoesis. In our study, which focusses on authority building, it would be tautological to try to identify authorisation (see Vaara and Tienari 2008; Reshef and Keim 2014). Also, the previously identified mechanisms of mythopoesis (Van Leeuwen 2007; Van Leeuwen and Wodak 1999; Vaara 2014; Reshef and Keim 2014) or narrativisation (Vaara and Tienari 2008; Thompson 1990) would require another level or type of analysis, since news writing takes basically the form of storytelling. As it regards rationalisation (Van Leeuwen 2007; Van Leeuwen and Wodak 1999; Vaara and Tienari 2008; Vaara 2014; Thompson 1990; Reshef and Keim 2014), it is treated in this study as a mechanism serving the two overarching legitimation discourses of objectivation and naturalisation. In other words, in this study objectivation and naturalisation are approached as discourses that are served by numerous modalities, mechanisms, and strategies, with rationalisation being one of them (see Table 4.1). Furthermore, our analytical framework has substantial differences from pre-existing models as it broadens the scope of analysis to include the investigation of journalistic practice, associated with its broader socio-political environment, as well as the dual logic of news, as facts and as stories. In that respect, it brings into the analysis the cultural studies approach on (the ideological implications of) narrative and journalistic authority (Zelizer 1992).

As already mentioned, the main discourses of legitimation are served by a variety of legitimising modalities, mechanisms, strategies, and practices, which can be identified in the texts' use of language, in their overall structure, in the journalistic practices that relate to the production of these texts, and in their broader context (which can be social, cultural, historical, or political). A discourse analysis narrowly focussed on the texts' linguistic features often fails to capture not only the texts' structures of meaning and ideology, but also their relations to the broader social context, as the latter are not always visible and explicit, but can be hidden, implied or even absent (and significant due to their absence). This is why CDA, supported by a cultural studies approach on text, is considered suitable for this study. Furthermore, this study moves beyond a narrowly focussed micro-textual analysis in order to identify discourse that is seen not only as language but as practice (which is performed through language). This is why all three dimensions – text, journalistic practice, and social practice – are examined in order to identify discourse.

Objectivation and naturalisation

According to Berger and Luckmann (1967, 78), objectivation is "the process by which the externalized products of human activity attain the character of objectivity". Language is one of the main instruments of objectivation. It objectivises the social experiences and the definitions of social reality by making them "available to all within the linguistic community, thus becoming both the basis and the instrument of the collective stock of knowledge" (ibid., 85–6). The institutionalisation of this "collective stock of knowledge", through the fields of education, religion, or science, facilitates to a large extent the objectivation of knowledge. Especially when it comes to knowledge that is a product of scientific or expert activity, it tends to take on the character of unquestioned objectivity, treated as ultimate truth.

For the purposes of our study, objectivation relates to "the presentation and (re)construction of information and ideas as real and objective facts that cannot be contested, having a quasi-scientific ontological status" (Doudaki 2015, 10). Through the constituents of objectivation (expertise, quantification, and reification), specific interpretations of social experiences "get the stamp of neutral factuality and are presented as objective incontestable reality" (Doudaki 2018, 154). From the perspective of journalistic practice, objectivation serves the overarching journalistic norm of objectivity, under which complicated, contradictory, and uncomplete events need to be presented as factual, neutral information. At the level of social practice, the objectivation of crucial dimensions of the economic crisis in Greece helps in the creation and consolidation of the hegemonic neoliberal discourse of the crisis as an objective reality beyond contestation (Doudaki et al. 2016, 2019).

The second main legitimation discourse is that of naturalisation. Naturalisation can be seen as a "state of affairs" in which "a social and historical creation may be treated as a natural event or as the inevitable outcome of natural characteristics" (Thompson 1990, 66). It broadly relates to the ways in which the information, opinions, and ideas appearing in the news "become taken for granted and practically unquestioned" (Doudaki 2015, 5), become common sense, and are presented as some kind of self-explanatory truth (Reshef and Keim 2014, 192) as "the way to do things" or as "the way things are" (Tuchman 1978, 196).

A naturalised discourse, according to Hall (2005, 71), is "not grounded in nature" but produces "nature as a sort of guarantee of its truth". Naturalisation, Fairclough (2015, 113) argues, "is the royal road to common sense". Through naturalisation, dominant discourses "appear to lose their connection with particular ideologies and become the common-sense practice of the institutions which employ them" (ibid., 126). "The apparent emptying of the ideological content of discourses is, paradoxically, a fundamental ideological effect: ideology works through disguising its nature, pretending to be what it isn't" (ibid., 113–14). Through naturalisation, ideologies become invisible, rendered as background assumptions that provide the framework for very particular interpretations of the issues appearing in the news, treated as neutral and transparent, and not as value-laden and opaque, and passing thus as they are offered, unscrutinised and uncontested.

Through naturalisation and its constituents (symbolic annihilation, mystification, and moralisation), the hegemonic ideologies regarding issues of public concern – in this case the economic crisis – are normalised and treated as a natural given, while "diverging opinions and ideas within the discursive struggle over the crisis are neutralised" (Doudaki 2015, 5). From the perspective of journalistic practice, naturalisation helps to create the layer upon which facts are positioned to tell the story in meaningful ways, serving the storytelling function of news. Additionally, what cannot be easily presented as factual information is processed into becoming common-sense knowledge, or the foundation on which facts can be based to reconstruct the news story. At the level of social practice, the naturalised hegemonic discourse about the crisis creates "an inescapable reality on the conditions of the crisis and their optimal handling" (Doudaki 2018, 147).

Objectivation and naturalisation do not function in isolation but rather complement and strengthen each other, in the service of the factual/narrative logics of news. This dual logic, which is crystallised into aesthetic and professional values and practices, provides the ground for the construction of spaces for the legitimation not only of policies, actions, and authority positions of the involved actors in the creation of news – in this specific case the news sources – but also of journalists themselves. A detailed presentation of the constituents and mechanisms of objectivation and naturalisation will take place in Chapter 4.

A framework for identifying discourses of legitimation in the news

In summary, the integrated comprehensive model for the identification of discourses of legitimation incorporates the examination of legitimation discourse through the prism of the factual/narrative logic of news, examined in three interrelated areas: (a) the systematic analysis of news texts, focussing on the presence of news sources; (b) the analysis of the journalistic practices that relate to the construction of these news texts; and (c) the contextualisation of the analysis in its specific socio-political environment.

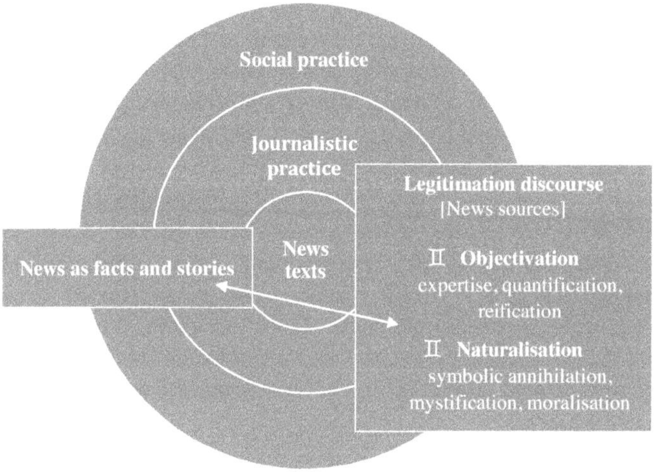

Figure 3.2 Identifying discourses of legitimation: levels and dimensions of analysis

Research methods and operationalisation

Before moving on to the presentation and elaboration of the study's findings, a brief account of the research methods and analytical process is pertinent.

This study examines news texts related to the three bailout agreements that Greece signed with the Troika, and the period around the completion of the terms of the third bailout agreement, which typically signifies the stabilisation of Greece's economy. It also examines the journalistic practices that relate to the production of news articles, together with the most important socio-political developments around the periods of study. For the purposes of research, each one of the study periods identified includes one week preceding and one week following the events related to the bailout agreements and the "green light" from creditors on the completion of the bailout agreement terms. More specifically, texts were selected from the following periods: 16 April – 10 May 2010 (first bailout agreement); 20 October 2011–19 February 2012, 29 April – 24 June 2012 (second bailout agreement); 18 January 2015–21 August 2015 (third bailout agreement); 14–28 June 2018 ("green light" on the completion of the terms of the third bailout) (for more information regarding the events during these periods, consult Chapter 1).

As the research focussed on "neutral" accounts of event reporting, only news reports were selected, while opinion articles, editorials, and other types of opinion-based texts were excluded. During the first stage of analysis, 50 texts were selected and coded to identify the main analytical categories and test the model. After the main analytical categories were detected and tested, 150 news articles were selected and analysed from the identified periods, 75 from *Ta Nea* and 75 from *I Kathimerini* (approximately 20 articles from each period, per newspaper). The texts to be analysed were selected through systematic random sampling from a pool of 3,612 news articles (1,768 from *Ta Nea* and 2,444 from *I Kathimerini*). This large group of articles had been located through a search in the print newspapers' online archives using the key words "Memorandum", "loan agreement", "bailout (programme/package)", "Troika", "IMF", "Eurogroup" (for 2018) – plus a number of other key words referring to Memoranda during 2010–2012, before the term "Memorandum" prevails – and comprise all the news reports that the two newspapers published on bailout-related events during the aforementioned periods.

The study focussed on the systematic and thorough examination of the news sources and their role in legitimating policies, actions, and authority positions. For the purposes of the study, we defined as a news source

> any individual, (representative of) organisation, or institution, appearing in the text giving information, position or opinion. A source can be named or unnamed, quoted in direct speech or mentioned in indirect speech by the journalist. An individual/organisation/institution appearing in the text only as agent who is involved in the story, without however providing information or opinion, is not considered a source but an actor.
>
> (Doudaki and Boubouka 2015)

The news texts selected were analysed following the principles of textual analysis, in order to identify the main legitimation discourses and their mechanisms.[7] The analysis followed the previously described framework for the identification of legitimation discourse. An open coding process (Saldaña 2009), instructed by the previous versions of the framework (Doudaki 2015, 2018), was implemented to explore the possibility of new categories inductively emerging from the data. The texts were coded by both researchers. Saturation regarding the main categories was reached rather early, approximately shortly after 40 articles were coded. Saturation regarding the texts' more elaborate features was reached approximately shortly after 75 articles were coded. The analysis confirmed the existence of the two overarching legitimation discourses of objectivation and naturalisation that had been identified in the previous studies. Also, a series of coding rounds, through an iterative process, allowed for the updated nalytical model to be enriched as it regards the mechanisms and modalities that serve the main legitimation discourses.

The analytical framework that was developed for the purposes of this study integrated one new dimension (in comparison to the previous studies): the factual/narrative nature of news. Furthermore, the updated analytical framework incorporated rather explicitly (which was not the case in the previous studies) the three levels of analysis – text, journalistic practice, social practice – that are informed by the principles of CDA (Fairclough 1992, 2015).

As was already mentioned and will be elaborated throughout the analysis, objectivation comprises expertise, quantification, and reification, while naturalisation consists of symbolic annihilation (omission, trivialisation, and condemnation), mystification, and moralisation. The study explores how objectivation and naturalisation help to legitimate policies and positions of authority, via the use of sources in the news texts studied. The analysis presents and discusses examples from all periods of study, from both newspapers, relating them to the journalistic practices that instructed their creation, as well as their socio-political context, accommodating in the analysis the specificity and contingency of social practice. All news article excerpts used as examples in the analysis have been translated from Greek into English.

Notes

1 The development of the objectivity norm reflects also the pursuit for internal social control in the news organisation, which aims at securing that journalists will be delivering news not only along the lines of professionalism but also within the line of the news organisation's policy (Tuchman 1972; Schudson 2001), which is not a focus of this study.
2 The famous assertion "comment is free, but facts are sacred" is attributed to CP Scott, editor of the *Manchester Guardian*, in his leading article on the centenary of the newspaper, in May 1921. See: www.theguardian.com/sustainability/cp-scott-centenary-essay.
3 See also Anstead and Chadwick's work (2018, 251) on "authority signaling", which the authors define as "a process whereby journalists, politicians and activists define and share information from expert sources in ways that enhance theirs and the expert source's status, legitimacy and ultimately power".
4 It should be noted that Gramsci did not exclude force entirely. He argued: "The 'normal' exercise of hegemony [. . .] is characterized by the combination of force and consent variously balancing one another, without force exceeding consent too much" (Gramsci 1999, 261).
5 See Peters's (1966) work on the authority of the teacher.
6 Source: Ministry of Interior of Greece. http://ekloges-prev.singularlogic.eu/v2009/pages/index.html?lang=en
7 The analysis also included a quantitative content analysis to identify the sources' main characteristics (i.e. number and identity of sources) and some of the texts' formal features in relation to the presence of sources in the news texts (the findings of which are part of a separate study). The quantitative content analysis of the 150 news articles identified 1,086 news sources in total.

References

Abbott, Andrew D. 1988. *The System of Professions: An Essay on the Division of Expert Labor*. Chicago: University of Chicago Press.

Althusser, Louis. 1971. *Lenin and Philosophy and Other Essays*. London: New Left.

Anstead, Nici, and Andrew Chadwick. 2018. "A Primary Definer Online: The Construction and Propagation of a Think Tank's Authority on Social Media." *Media, Culture & Society* 40 (2): 246–66.

Bates, Thomas R. 1975. "Gramsci and the Theory of Hegemony." *Journal of the History of Ideas* 36 (2): 351–66.

Baym, Geoffrey. 2000. "Constructing Moral Authority: We in the Discourse of Television News." *Western Journal of Communication* 64 (1): 92–111.

Berger, Peter L., and Thomas Luckmann. 1967. *The Social Construction of Reality*. London: Penguin Books.

Berkowitz, Dan. 2009. "Reporters and Their Sources." In *The Handbook of Journalism Studies*, edited by Karin Wahl-Jorgensen and Thomas Hanitzsch, 102–15. New York: Routledge.

Bird, Elizabeth S., and Robert W. Dardenne. 1988. "Myth, Chronicle, and Story: Exploring the Narrative Qualities of News." In *Media, Myth, and Narratives: Television and the Press*, edited by James W. Carey, 67–86. Newbury Park, CA: Sage.

Buozis, Michael, and Brian Creech. 2018. "Reading News as Narrative: A Genre Approach to Journalism Studies." *Journalism Studies* 19 (10): 1430–46.

Buzzelli, Cary, and Bill Johnston. 2001. "Authority, Power, and Morality in Classroom Discourse." *Teaching and Teacher Education* 17 (8): 873–84.

Carpentier, Nico, and Benjamin De Cleen. 2007. "Bringing Discourse Theory into Media Studies: The Applicability of Discourse Theoretical Analysis (DTA) for the Study of Media Practises and Discourses." *Journal of Language and Politics* 6 (2): 265–93.

Carragee, Kevin M., and Wim Roefs. 2004. "The Neglect of Power in Recent Framing Research." *Journal of Communication* 54 (2): 214–33.

Deetz, Stanley. 1977. *Democracy in an Age of Corporate Colonization*. Albany, NY: State University of New York Press.

Doudaki, Vaia. 2015. "Legitimation Mechanisms in the Bailout Discourse." *Javnost: The Public* 22 (1): 1–17.

Doudaki, Vaia, and Angeliki Boubouka. 2015. "Coding and Textual Analysis Synoptic Guide." Unpublished document.

Doudaki, Vaia. 2018. "Discourses of Legitimation in the News: The Case of the Cypriot Bailout." In *Cyprus and Its Conflicts: Representations, Materialities and Cultures*, edited by Vaia Doudaki and Nico Carpentier, 142–62. New York: Berghahn Books.

Doudaki, Vaia, Angeliki Boubouka, Lia-Paschalia Spyridou, and Christos Tzalavras. 2016. "Dependency, (Non)Liability and Austerity News Frames of Bailout Greece." *European Journal of Communication* 31 (4): 426–45.

Doudaki, Vaia, Angeliki Boubouka, and Christos Tzalavras. 2019. "Framing the Cypriot Financial Crisis: In the Service of the Neoliberal Vision." *Journalism* 20 (2): 349–68.

Dow, Bonnie J. 1990. "Hegemony, Feminist Criticism and the *Mary Tyler Moore Show*." *Critical Studies in Mass Communication* 7 (3): 261–74.
Dowling, John, and Jeffrey Pfeffer. 1975. "Organizational Legitimacy: Social Values and Organizational Behavior." *Pacific Sociological Review* 18 (1): 122–36.
Fairclough, Norman. 1992. *Discourse and Social Change*. Cambridge: Polity Press.
Fairclough, Norman. 2003. *Analysing Discourse: Textual Analysis for Social Research*. London: Longman.
Fairclough, Norman. 2015. *Language and Power*. 3rd ed. New York: Routledge.
Figdor, Carrie. 2010. "Is Objective News Possible?" In *Journalism Ethics: A Philosophical Approach*, edited by Christopher Meyers, 153–64. New York: Oxford University Press.
Foucault, Michel. 1972. *The Archaeology of Knowledge*. Translated by Alan M. Sheridan Smith. New York: Pantheon.
Gitlin, Todd. 1980. *The Whole World Is Watching: Mass Media in the Making and Unmaking of the New Left*. Berkeley: University of California Press.
Gramsci, Antonio. 1971. *Selections from the Prison Notebooks*. New York: International Publishers.
Gramsci, Antonio. 1999. *The Antonio Gramsci Reader: Selected Writings 1916–1935*. Edited by David Forgacs. London: Lawrence and Wishart.
Gunster, Shane, and Paul Saurette. 2014. "Storylines in the Sands: News, Narrative, and Ideology in the Calgary Herald." *Canadian Journal of Communication* 39 (3): 333–59.
Hall, Peter A. 2018. "Varieties of Capitalism in Light of the Euro Crisis." *Journal of European Public Policy* 25 (1): 7–30.
Hall, Stuart. 1979. "Culture, the Media, and the 'Ideological Effect'." In *Mass Communication and Society*, edited by James Curran, Michael Gurevitch, and Janet Woollacott, 315–48. Beverly Hills, CA: Sage.
Hall, Stuart. 2005. "The Rediscovery of 'Ideology': Return of the Repressed in Media Studies." In *Culture, Society and the Media*, edited by Michael Gurevitch, Tony Bennett, James Curran, and Janet Woollacott, 52–86. London: Routledge.
Hall, Stuart, Chas Critcher, Tony Jefferson, John Clarke, and Brian Roberts. 1978. *Policing the Crisis: Mugging, the State, and Law and Order*. New York: Palgrave Macmillan.
Harvey, David. 2005. *A Brief History of Neoliberalism*. Oxford: Oxford University Press.
Hiotis, Vasilis. 2015. "Δημοσκόπηση: Προβάδισμα 'Ναι' σε Δημοψήφισμα, πριν τη 'Βόμβα Τσίπρα'." *To Vima*, 27 June. www.tovima.gr/2015/06/27/politics/dimoskopisi-probadisma-nai-se-dimopsifisma-prin-ti-bomba-tsipra/.
Iyengar, Shanto. 1994. *Is Anyone Responsible? How Television Frames Political Issues*. Chicago: University of Chicago Press.
Jørgensen, Marianne W., and Louise J. Phillips. 2002. *Discourse Analysis as Theory and Method*. London: Sage.
Laclau, Ernesto, and Chantal Mouffe. 1985. *Hegemony and Socialist Strategy: Towards a Radical Democratic Politics*. London: Verso.

Lindblom, Charles. 1977. *Politics and Markets: The World's Political-Economic Systems*. New York: Basic Books.

Lippmann, Walter. 1920. *Liberty and the News*. New York: Harcourt, Brace and Howe.

McQuail, Denis. 1992. *Media Performance: Mass Communication and the Public Interest*. London: Sage.

McQuail, Denis. 2013. *Journalism and Society*. London: Sage.

Pagoulatos, George. 2018. *Greece after the Bailouts: Assessment of a Qualified Failure*. Hellenic Observatory Discussion Papers on Greece and Southeast Europe. GreeSE Paper No. 130. www.lse.ac.uk/Hellenic-Observatory/Assets/Documents/Publications/GreeSE-Papers/GreeSE-No130.pdf.

Papavlassopoulos, Efthimis. 2015. "Μετατοπίσεις στο Ελληνικό Κομματικό Σύστημα: Από το Ενιαίο Μαζικό Κόμμα του Κράτους στο Κόμμα 'Εκτάκτου Εθνικής Ανάγκης'; [Transformations and Shifts in the Greek Party System: From the Mass Party of the State to the 'National Emergency Party'?]." In *Το Πολιτικό Πορτραίτο της Ελλάδας [The Political Portrait of Greece]*, edited by Nikos G. Georgarakis and Nicolas Demertzis, 141–67. Athens: Gutenberg Editions and National Centre for Social Research.

Peters, Richard Stanley. 1966. *Ethics and Education*. London: Allen & Unwin.

Reese, Stephen D. 1990. "The News Paradigm and the Ideology of Objectivity: A Socialist at the Wall Street Journal." *Critical Studies in Media Communication* 7 (4): 390–409.

Reshef, Yonatan, and Charles Keim. 2014. *Bad Time Stories: Government-Union Conflicts and the Rhetoric of Legitimation Strategies*. Toronto: University of Toronto Press.

Richardson, Alan John. 1985. "Symbolic and Substantive Legitimation in Professional Practice." *Canadian Journal of Sociology/Cahiers canadiens de sociologie* 10 (2): 139–52.

Rojo, Luisa Martín, and Teun A. van Dijk. 1997. "'There Was a Problem, and It Was Solved!': Legitimating the Expulsion of 'Illegal' Migrants in Spanish Parliamentary Discourse." *Discourse & Society* 8 (4): 523–66.

Saldaña, Johnny. 2009. *The Coding Manual for Qualitative Researchers*. London: Sage.

Schudson, Michael. 1978. *Discovering the News: A Social History of American Newspapers*. New York: Basic Books.

Schudson, Michael. 1982. "The Politics of Narrative Form: The Emergence of News Conventions in Print and Television." *Daedalus* 111 (4): 97–112.

Schudson, Michael. 1995. *The Power of News*. Cambridge, MA: Harvard University Press.

Schudson, Michael. 2001. "The Objectivity Norm in American Journalism." *Journalism* 2 (2): 149–70.

Schudson, Michael, and Chris Anderson. 2009. "Objectivity, Professionalism, and Truth Seeking in Journalism." In *The Handbook of Journalism Studies*, edited by Karin Wahl-Jorgensen and Thomas Hanitzsch, 88–101. New York: Routledge.

Schultz, Julianne. 1998. *Reviving the Fourth Estate: Democracy, Accountability and the Media*. Cambridge: Cambridge University Press.

Scott, John. 2001. *Power*. Cambridge: Polity Press.
Sigal, Leon V. 1986. "Who? Sources Make the News." In *Reading the News*, edited by Robert Karl Manoff and Michael Schudson, 9–37. New York: Pantheon Books.
Soloski, John. 1989. "News Reporting and Professionalism: Some Constraints on the Reporting of the News." *Media, Culture & Society* 11 (2): 207–28.
Spady, William G., and Douglas E. Mitchell. 1979. "Authority and the Management of Classroom Activities." In *Classroom Management*, edited by Daniel L. Duke, 75–115. National Society for the Study of Education. Chicago, IL: University of Chicago Press.
Suchman, Mark C. 1995. "Managing Legitimacy: Strategic and Institutional Approaches." *Academy of Management Review* 20 (3): 571–610.
Thompson, John B. 1990. *Ideology and Modern Culture: Critical Social Theory in the Era of Mass Communication*. Cambridge: Polity Press.
Torfing, Jacob. 1999. *New Theories of Discourse*. Oxford: Blackwell Publishers.
Tuchman, Gaye. 1972. "Objectivity as Strategic Ritual: An Examination of Newsmen's Notions of Objectivity." *American Journal of Sociology* 77 (4): 660–79.
Tuchman, Gaye. 1978. *Making News: A Study in the Construction of Reality*. New York: Free Press.
Tziovaras, Gregoris. 2015. "Γκάλοπ ALCO: 57% να Υπογράψουν κι ας Είναι και Μνημόνιο!." *Protothema.gr*. 28 June. www.protothema.gr/politics/article/488501/57-na-upograpsoun-ki-as-einai-kai-mnimonio/.
Vaara, Eero. 2014. "Struggles over Legitimacy in the Eurozone Crisis: Discursive Legitimation Strategies and Their Ideological Underpinnings." *Discourse & Society* 25 (4): 500–18.
Vaara, Eero, and Janne Tienari. 2008. "A Discursive Perspective on Legitimation Strategies in Multinational Corporations." *Academy of Management Review* 33 (4): 985–93.
Van Gorp, Baldwin. 2007. "The Constructionist Approach to Framing: Bringing Culture Back in." *Journal of Communication* 57 (1): 60–78.
Van Gorp, Baldwin. 2010. "Strategies to Take Subjectivity out of Framing Analysis." In *Doing News Framing Analysis: Empirical and Theoretical Perspectives*, edited by Paul D'Angelo and Jim A. Kuypers, 84–109. New York: Routledge.
Van Leeuwen, Theo. 2007. "Legitimation in Discourse and Communication." *Discourse & Communication* 1 (1): 91–112.
Van Leeuwen, Theo, and Ruth Wodak. 1999. "Legitimizing Immigration Control: A Discourse-Historical Analysis." *Discourse Studies* 1 (1): 83–118.
Ward, Stephen J.A. 2010. "Inventing Objectivity: New Philosophical Foundations." In *Journalism Ethics: A Philosophical Approach*, edited by Christopher Meyers, 137–52. New York: Oxford University Press.
Weber, Max. 1978. *Economy and Society*. Edited by Guenther Roth and Claus Wittich. Berkeley: University of California Press.
Weber, Max. 2015. "Politics as Vocation." In *Weber's Rationalism and Modern Society*, edited and translated by Tony Waters and Dagmar Waters, 129–98. New York: Palgrave Macmillan.

Westerståhl, Jörgen. 1983. "Objective News Reporting: General Premises." *Communication Research* 10 (3): 403–24.
Williams, Raymond. 1977. *Marxism and Literature*. New York: Oxford University Press.
Willis, Paul. 1977. *Learning to Labour: How Working-Class Kids Get Working-Class Jobs*. Franborough: Saxon House.
Zelizer, Barbie. 1992. *Covering the Body: The Kennedy Assassination, the Media, and the Shaping of Collective Memory*. Chicago: University of Chicago Press.
Zelizer, Barbie. 2004. "When Facts, Truth, and Reality Are God-Terms: On Journalism's Uneasy Place in Cultural Studies." *Communication and Critical/Cultural Studies* 1 (1): 100–19.

4 Analysing discourse

Legitimation and its mechanisms in the Greek bailout news

Vaia Doudaki

This chapter presents and elaborates on the discourses of legitimation, as they have been identified through the analysis of the two newspapers' articles and their related journalistic practices. Throughout the chapter, texts from the analysed material will be used to exemplify the analysis. This chapter discusses how the two overarching discourses of objectivation and naturalisation, and their constituents (see Table 4.1), are put into effect in order to legitimate or delegitimate actions, policies, ideologies, and the authority positions of the involved actors and of the journalists themselves. The analysis brings together the various constituents and dimensions (text, journalistic practice, and broader context), in order to investigate discourse not strictly as language but as (social) practice. The combined CDA-cultural studies approach to the analysis allows for the exploration of the ideological implications of legitimation discourse, relating them to the factual/narrative logic of news.

Table 4.1 Discourses of legitimation and their mechanisms

Objectivation	*Naturalisation*
Expertise Individuals /institutions recognised as possessing advanced knowledge, are used to present, support or contest decisions, actions, policies, over a domain or issue.	**Symbolic annihilation (omission, trivialisation, condemnation)** **Omission:** Important information for the comprehension of an issue is missing. **Trivialisation**: Important information is treated as trivial, of minor importance, or already presented (and thus not necessary to be explained). **Condemnation**: An actor, practice, decision is critiqued as wrong, harmful, disastrous, unethical.

(*Continued*)

Table 4.1 (Continued)

Objectivation	*Naturalisation*
Quantification Dates and numbers are used to articulate arguments, support views and policies; data are used as tools of persuasion.	**Mystification** Insinuations and half-explained or blackboxed information create a blurred or obscure discursive environment; a lot is left unclear, vagueness prevails; processes and practices are concealed.
Reification Institutions and political actions appear as autonomous entities and not as products of human activity; individuals are dissociated from the activities they are involved in; while individuals lose agency, the products of human activity gain agency.	**Moralisation** Language evoking moral codes and values is used to describe a situation or phenomenon; value-laden language is aimed at creating positive or negative moral connotations for people, actions, and decisions.

Mechanisms and modalities serving both discourses

Rationalisation (mainly through):

- Obligation modalities (*must, should*, etc.)
- Definition modalities (*is, constitutes, means*, etc.)
- Explanation modalities (*because*, etc.)
- Predictions and hypotheses

Nominalisation: Language entailing activity/agency (e.g. phrases/verbs describing actions) is expressed through nouns.

Passivisation: Verbs are presented in passive form.

Displacement: An object/term/human being is used to refer to another, transferring its (positive or negative) qualities to the latter.

Euphemisation: Actions/institutions are described in terms that create positive value.

Dissimulation: Events/processes are represented in ways that deflect attention from actual practice.

Eternalisation: Actions/phenomena are disconnected from their historical/temporal dimensions.

Unification: People are categorised under a common trait/identity, disregarding differences/divisions.

Fragmentation and differentiation: Focus on groups' and individuals' differences, highlighting what divides and disunites them.

Expurgation of the other: Groups and individuals are portrayed as dangerous, harmful, evil.

Discourse of objectivation

Objectivation, as already explained, concerns the presentation of information and ideas in the news as real, objective, incontestable facts, often disguising their contingent and ideological nature and implications. At the level of journalistic practice, objectivation serves the logics of objectivity, under which complex events and ideologically charged positions need to be presented as neutral, factual information. As the textual analysis shows, objectivation is performed through the mechanisms of expertise, quantification, and reification that were employed by journalists and their sources in the news texts covering the economic crisis in Greece.

Expertise

Expertise is related to the recognised possession of advanced or sophisticated knowledge over a domain, field, discipline, or science. Through the performance of knowledge, experts do not simply communicate information; they communicate information organised in suggested frameworks of meaning, offering proposed "ways of knowing" (Rose 1990, ix) and recommending what the significance or relevance of that information is. This is of particular importance for societies that struggle to manage an environment of constant volatility and contingency. Experts and centres of expertise are hence seen as centres of stabilised knowledge, invoked in an attempt "to know and manage the uncertain in the name of certainty" (Kelly 2000, 312). Expertise has thus a tacit disciplining power, "enacting assorted attempts at the calculated administration of diverse aspects of conduct through countless, often competing, local tactics of education, persuasion, inducement, management, incitement, motivation and encouragement" (Rose and Miller 1992, 175).

Journalism can be seen as a field of expertise itself, to the degree that it has been recognised as the domain with jurisdiction over the collection and dissemination of information about current events, in the form of news. At the same time, connoisseurs from other fields are frequently used as news sources, especially "since they are seen as combining the qualities of knowledge and independence. They are able to provide expert or scientific knowledge, which journalists often lack, and are considered unattached to specific interests" (Doudaki 2015, 11). Expert authority is also not easy to contest; thus, through the presence of connoisseurs, the journalistic work is granted more easily the stamp of objectivity. As it regards the economic crisis in Greece, economy and market experts are regularly invited to offer their suggested "ways of knowing" (Rose 1990, ix) about the crisis and its constituents. The media depends on experts to a greater extent during critical moments, such as those related to the bailout agreements and their implications, because during these times the degree of uncertainty over their outcomes is considerably high.

The following example from our analysis comes from the time when the Greek government agreed to the terms of the second bailout programme with the Troika partners, in February 2012, in return for new austerity measures. The opinion of a bank executive is treated as fact by the journalist, in this celebratory, non-critical article, which starts as follows:

> The countdown for the sanitisation of the banking system with the recapitalisation of banks and the radical treatment of the problematic elements of the balance sheets, has begun. By the end of September, when the great project of recapitalisation will have been completed, we will essentially have a new banking system free from the great ordeal of excessive exposure to Greek government bonds, but also from the uncertainty that was caused by the loan portfolio and the financing of many companies . . . with questionable banking criteria.
>
> (*I Kathimerini*, 08.02.2012).

The opinion of the bank executive, which follows in the second paragraph, does not differ at all in terms of style and argumentation from the journalist's lead: "'This autumn', a bank executive stresses, 'we will be talking about a new banking system, as the two main concerns of the markets, the exposure to bonds and the status of loan portfolios will have been definitely addressed'". Definite statements about the future ("By the end of September [. . .] we will essentially have" or "This autumn we will be talking about a new banking system [. . .] as the concerns of the markets will have been definitely addressed") serve to rationalise predictions and elevate them to the level of (eventual) fact. The token of objectivity is strengthened by the use of the expert's words of wisdom, which are treated as facts and presented by the journalist in a neutral and detached fashion, and thus as truth statements, and not as a product of evaluation and prioritisation.

In the following example, analysts legitimate the agreement terms regarding the upcoming "exodus" of the Greek economy from the third Memorandum, on August 2018, through a there-is-no-alternative (TINA) argument:

> It could not have been different, analysts say, noting that the country does not convince that it will continue its reforming dynamics and fiscal discipline if this is not imposed from above. The "enhanced supervision", as opposed to the simple post-Memorandum monitoring, lenders themselves maintain, is fair, given the large amount of loans given to the country. Perhaps, moreover, some analysts note, the "supervision" itself is not bad after all, to the degree that it imposes the necessary

> discipline. However, the obligation to keep high primary surpluses for such a long time is considered problematic. "With such high surpluses we will not see growth", an analyst is commenting.
>
> (*I Kathimerini*, 25a.06.2018)[1]

Analysts use moralising language here, describing the deal as "fair" and "not bad", and rationalise it through definition and explanation modalities ("The 'enhanced supervision' [. . .] is fair *given* the large amount of loans"; "it imposes the *necessary* discipline [that Greece lacks]"). Some of the negative sides of the deal appear in the same paragraph, but they are downplayed, and even if they are severe (for example, the obligation of high primary surpluses for many years has been considered unrealistic by many politicians, economists, and market experts), they are presented at the end of the paragraph and thus evaluated as being less important. Still, it should be acknowledged that the article is overall critical about the terms of completion of the third bailout programme, pointing to the harsh obligations and risks for the Greek economy in the post-Memorandum era. At the same time, however, the critical tone does not overrule the TINA logic, brought through the expert source in the article.

The following article comes from the same period of negotiations with the EU partners regarding the post-Memorandum terms Greece has to abide by. Experts are invoked to legitimate the fact that the plan – which was suggested by France and would have been beneficial for Greece as it could have mitigated the risks related to the country's high debt – was severely critisised by Germany and was finally rejected. The excerpt's emphasis, deployed through rationalised arguments, is on the benefits of the deal for investors and for the markets:

> The game has not ended for Greece . . . but only its first half, economists say in "Kathimerini", commenting on Eurogroup's decisions. They are talking about a deal that was the best that the country could get at this moment, which gives investors visibility and reduces the risk related to the Greek government bonds, even if the plans to apply the "French mechanism" which is considered to be a more powerful tool for improving the loan condition of Greece, were abandoned.
>
> (*I Kathimerini*, 25b.06.2018)

In most cases, the use of economic and financial experts is highly instrumental. They are invited by journalists on the basis of their degree of authority and/or the journalists' assumptions about the interpretative framework they are going to offer. Thus, they do not appear as primary generators of events, but – being asked to provide the interpretative framework of events and act as knowledge stabilisers – they function rather as meta-actors in the news. At the same time, the products of expertise by market and bank specialists (e.g. forecast reports on the performance of national economies, of market sectors, shares, and their related rating apparatuses) are treated more and more as news, not merely as products of expertise. In this manner they acquire a factual status beyond their value as predictions or estimations. In addition, they are dissociated from their producers, appearing as created on their own and not by humans. This function is related to the reification of the markets, which is explained later in this chapter.

It is worth noting that in none of the articles examined the interpretative framework offered by an expert is scrutinised by the journalist. Rather the views of experts, which are very often highly speculative, are treated as objective reality, either implicitly or explicitly. In the cases in which the opinions of several experts are hosted in one article, the ones that are closer to the journalist's and the newspaper's position are prioritised, whilst the ones that diverge are downplayed or trivialised.

Through the use of expertise, decisions and policies related to the bail-out agreements are evaluated in the news as well thought out, planned, or executed, based on scientific and sophisticated tools and criteria that are supposed to limit the risk of failure. The signifying practice of expertise also assists in the legitimation of positions and authority building of the involved political and other institutional actors (e.g. of the EU or IMF), since the views and actions of the latter are supported by the interpretative framework offered by the experts; of the experts themselves, as their presence in the news helps to establish and maintain their role as connoisseurs; and of the journalists and the news media they work for, as their work is given the stamp of objectivity through the presence of experts in their news stories.

Quantification

Quantification, the act of systematic counting and measuring, is considered fundamental for the sciences, as it is seen as one of the main ways of consistently observing, registering, and interpreting (our observations about) our environment. Relatedly, the development of methods and techniques of quantitatively measuring, reporting, and explaining – largely through statistics – social phenomena and behaviour, is considered to contribute to objectivity in the social sciences (Porter 1995; Smith 1994).

When it comes to news and journalism, the systematic use of data in the news is seen as one of the core elements of objective journalism: what can be closer to hard facts than data, and especially numbers? However, data are often used in the news, not merely as carriers of the information that is necessary for the comprehension of the issue that is being presented, but in strategic and instrumental ways to support certain arguments and positions, and discredit others (Doudaki 2015, 12–3, 2018, 156–7). Within this logic, quantification in the news refers to the use of numbers and data "more as tools of persuasion than aids to comprehension" (Goddard 1998, 87).

In the example of quantification that follows, the first Minister of Finance of the Syriza government, Yanis Varoufakis, is trying to explain the newly elected government's position during the negotiations with the Troika in March 2015, using emotional language and quantified arguments:

> "The Memorandum was and remains toxic. What percentage of the Memorandum do we accept? Exactly zero percent. We do not accept even one condition that leads to new taxes and salary reductions". He also added that the government cannot tolerate "a single line" that would involve new sacrifices for Greeks. "We will keep the parts that they [the Troika] had proposed and which do not threaten to infect the new agreement. For example, why reject the commitment to reform the tax code? Or, to redefine the concept of tax evasion? 70% of the fig leaf is either of no significance or irrelevant to the Memorandum's logic", Mr. Varoufakis continued, and concluded: "I repeat that we accept 0% of the Memorandum. What percentage of the measures do we accept? Around 30% is the toxic part of the Memorandum that we will reject".
>
> (*I Kathimerini*, 11.02.2015)

The Minister of Finance attempts, in this example, to reconcile and legitimate the rhetoric of rejecting the Memorandum, which was the flagship of Syriza's pre-electoral campaign, with the negotiation – and in practice later acceptance – of the great majority of its measures, by actually avoiding to give precise information about what the government will actually accept. Mr. Varoufakis (who is a professor of economics) is combining in his rhetoric a moralising and emotionally charged tone ("toxic Memorandum", "the government cannot tolerate 'a single line' that would involve new sacrifices for the Greeks") that is rationalised through percentages and definition modalities ("we accept 0% of the Memorandum", "the Memorandum was and remains toxic"). This rhetoric, combined also with the strategy of asking questions himself (setting thus the framework) and then answering these questions (within the framework that he set by himself) (e.g. "What percentage of the Memorandum do we accept? Exactly zero percent."), which was consistently used by Varoufakis during the time he was a Finance Minister,[2] attempts to establish authority through agency, and to communicate that the Syriza government is powerful and in the position to set its own terms.

The following example of quantification comes from March 2015, when the European partners were putting pressure on the new Syriza government to stick to the previously agreed reforms, in this case by limiting the liquidity available to Greek banks. In order to support his position that the ECB had been helping Greece more than any other European country, the president of ECB,

> Mr. Draghi reacted strongly to the criticism by members of the European Parliament that he is blackmailing Greece. He reiterated that the total exposure of the ECB in Greece reaches today €104 billion or 64% of Greek GDP, whereas three months ago (in December),[3] the exposure was only €50 billion. "This is the country where the ECB has the greatest exposure", he said.
>
> (*I Kathimerini*, 24.03.2015)

Similarly, the extent to which Greece has been assisted by European institutions is quantitatively used to legitimate – and rationalise through explanation and confirmation modalities ("due to", "obviously", "indeed", "thus") – the reason why Greece will be under tight supervision after completing the terms of the third Memorandum in August 2018. The European official quoted in the following article is using a moralising argument ("Europeans will be by Greece's side") to soften the tight supervision clause:

> Europeans will be by Greece's side until 2059, when the last instalment of loans to the ESM [European Stability Mechanism] will be repaid, noted ESM chief Klaus Regling, speaking at the Economist conference, adding that supervision "will obviously be tighter due to the height of loans and debt relief". Indeed, yesterday, just after the multi-bill was ratified, ESM approved the disbursement of the €1bn instalment that was pending from the third evaluation. Thus, ESM's total financial assistance in the current programme [of financial support] towards Greece will reach €46.9 billion, out of the €86 billion that is available. Overall, the ESM and the European Financial Stability Facility (EFSF) have so far disbursed to Greece nearly €189 billion.
>
> (*Ta Nea*, 15.06.2018)

It should be acknowledged that the article overall is sceptical towards the terms of the "exodus" agreement. It points to the dangers and risks that the deal entails – without, however, seriously questioning it – as there are no suggestions of any alternatives. The frame that the article employs combines the TINA logic with the argument that the creditors are in full control. The focus is on the tight supervision of the Greek economy and on the dangers of Greece derailing from the terms laid out by the deal. This framing is used to undermine Syriza's policy, as it becomes clear from the article's lead, where it is stated that the "Greek economy will be found in a tight surveillance tunnel for many years [. . .] deconstructing the government's narrative of a 'clean exit' from the Memoranda." Furthermore, the government's perspective on the terms of the agreement is presented only at the end of the article, and it is rather disconnected from the rest of the text, both in content and in tone.

The effectiveness of quantification is enhanced when it is combined with expertise: When experts employ quantified arguments, it becomes hard to contest these assertions, especially since they are rarely (counter)balanced by alternative ones. In the following example, a quantified argument, supported by a confirmation modality ("of course"), is used to legitimate the terms of the agreement related to the "exodus" from the Memoranda that was reached with the EU partners, framing it as positive for Greece. What is omitted, from the market source's quantified argument, is what the obligations of the country will be after 2032:

> No one doubts, of course, that extending the EFSF loans and the period of grace for their interest rates over a 10-year period is a positive fact. They may have hoped, at the Ministry of Finance, until a few months ago, for a 15-year extension, but 10 years are also considered satisfactory. Until 2032, we will not pay anything for about a third of our loans, a source of the bond market points out.
>
> (*I Kathimerini*, 25a.06.2018)

Still, later on in the same paragraph, a professor explains that the success of the deal is conditional on several important factors:

> As Professor Panagiotis Petrakis explains, "debt is sustainable in the medium term for a decade but under normal conditions and subject to the primary surplus targets. If, instead of achieving the target of 3.5% of GDP, we are down to 3% of GDP, the situation changes drastically. Therefore, uncertainty will not disappear."

As it is shown in the analysis, the strategic use of numbers and other data aids the legitimation of economic policy decisions and measures. At the same time, the discursive practice of quantification helps to maintain the authority positions of the actors involved – both sources and journalists – as it creates a shield of objectification by means of the supposedly incontestable force of numbers, which are treated as facts that are hard to contest. The logic and practice of quantification is efficient because in most cases the numbers evoked are correct in absolute terms. However, they are detached from their context and are dissociated from the actors who have decided upon and implemented them; in some cases, they are even put in other contexts proposing new associations and interpretations. From this perspective, quantification is closely related to omission and reification.

Reification

Berger and Luckmann (1967, 106) argue that "[r]eification is the apprehension of human phenomena as if they were things, that is, in non-human or possibly suprahuman terms". Through reification, the individual is disconnected from his/her "own authorship of the human world", and the world is experienced as an external, dehumanised facticity, over which the individual has no control. The authors see reification "as an extreme step in the process of objectivation, whereby the objectivised world loses its comprehensibility as a human enterprise and becomes fixated as a non-human, non-humanizable, inert facticity" (ibid.).[4] Thompson argues that reification involves the representation of

> a transitory, historical state of affairs as if it were permanent, natural, outside of time. Processes are portrayed as things or as events of a quasi-natural kind, in such a way that involves the elimination or obfuscation of the social and historical character of social-historical phenomena.
>
> (1990, 65)

Through reification, the human being, as "the producer of a world, is apprehended as its product, and human activity as an epiphenomenon of non-human processes" (Berger and Luckmann 1967, 107). At the same time, institutions are bestowed with "an ontological status independent of human activity and signification" (ibid.), while the roles that individuals may assume in institutions are objectified and are "apprehended as an inevitable fate, for which the individual may disclaim responsibility" (ibid., 108). In that sense, individuals working for or representing institutions may be performing specific roles without assuming responsibility for their actions related to these roles.

Economy (and its related institutions) is among the areas of human activity that is systematically reified in representations by news media. Economic activity often appears in the news "as the product of forces outside human control" (Tuchman 1978a, 213). At the same time, entities such as the markets appear as autonomous organisms that lead their own lives, and not as products of human activity (Goddard 1998, 77).

Relatedly, political actors that appear in the news rather frequently invoke "the demands of the global capital markets and meagre [. . .] finances to justify the austerity measures they had inflicted – or were about to" (Reshef and Keim 2014, 75), and present human-created documents such as government budgets as independent entities that handcuff the hands of involved actors, including their own authors (ibid.).

In bailout-related news, the markets and their associated institutions are regularly presented as powerful and loaded with agency, as well as having feelings. In addition, the need to restore the markets' trust or to respond correctly to the markets' reactions appears to be of crucial importance for Greece's economic future. For example, in the article excerpt that was presented earlier as an example of expertise (*I Kathimerini*, 08.02.2012), the markets' concerns will be eased after the recapitalisation of banks is completed. In another case, Greece is presented as being "in the punitive discretion" of the markets (*Ta Nea*, 20b.06.2018). Also, an article from the June 2018 period that refers to the terms of the exodus from the third Memorandum mentions that "while markets are expected to be relieved by [the decision on] the tight corset of post-Memorandum surveillance, it is by no means certain that they will consider that a clear pathway for the Greek debt opens up in the long-term" (*Ta Nea*, 21c.06.2018).

The next article was published in November 2011, following the agreement on the second bailout programme and the resignation of Prime Minister George Papandreou (This was a period of increased uncertainty, as a new transitory government needed to be formed with the task to initiate the implementation of the bailout terms). In the following article excerpt, it is "the system" that is presented as an independent entity:

> However, bank executives warn that the system's strength is limited, and emphasise the urgent need to restore peace through concrete actions so as to liberate society from the fear of economic destruction and bankruptcy. They stress that the strength of society has weakened, as people have been under intense psychological pressure for many months. According to the latest available data by the Bank of Greece, at the end of August deposits amounted to €188.6 billion, showing losses of €20.9 billion since the beginning of the year. Compared to December 2009, outflows are close to €50 billion.
>
> (*I Kathimerini*, 08.11.2011)

According to the bank executives cited in this article, society's liberation is dependent on the restoration of the system's strength. However, we are not informed which system is intended: One assumes from the article's context that it is the banking system, but through this vagueness the banking system and society are conflated, treated almost as one and the same. Moreover, while the first half of the paragraph is vague, void of a time frame and of human agency, the second half of the paragraph, which presents a series of data that cover a specific period of time, serves the legitimation of "the urgent need to restore the system's strength". Put differently, quantification comes to support reification through the additional BoG data that the journalist decides to present, associating them with the bank executives' arguments. Furthermore, through the narrow economistic logic that the journalist employs, the "strength of society" is measured by, or equalised with, the levels of its bank deposits.

Reification is often articulated through nominalisation and passivisation. In the first case, "sentences or part of sentences, descriptions of action and the participants involved in them, are turned into nouns" (Thompson 1990, 66), while in the second, verbs are presented in the passive form (ibid.) (e.g., "the markets' concerns will have been eased"). Nominalisation and passivisation "delete actors and agency and they tend to represent processes as things or events which take place in the absence of a subject who produces them", detached from their "specific spatial and temporal contexts" (ibid.). By "[r]epresenting process as thing, deleting actors and agency, constituting time as an eternal extension of the present tense" (ibid.), journalists reify the constituents and dimensions of the economic crisis and protect the involved actors by dissociating them from any responsibility.

As already mentioned in the section on expertise, reports regarding the economy are often treated as primary sources. We often find entire articles based exclusively on a single EU, IMF, or rating agency report. The following article from June 2018 (written prior to the "green light" by European partners on the completion of the third bailout requirements) serves as an example of this practice. The "Compliance Report" by the European Commission, following the fourth and final review regarding the degree of compliance of Greece to the terms of the bailout programme, is the article's unique source – and it is entirely objectified and given agency. While the report acquires agency, disconnected from any human association – as if it is not a product of human activity – its authors become invisible and therefore not responsible for its production (and the actions related to it):

> It is foreseen that "the completion of the fourth review of the ESM programme will contribute to a sustained improvement in business sentiment and Greece's ability to attract foreign investment", the report says, but also mentions the risks that the Greek economy may face in relation to investment financing and regional political developments. [. . .] As for the implementation of the privatisation programme, the report says that "the picture we have is mixed with progress in some areas and delays elsewhere". [. . .] "Should these four transactions [privatisations

> regarding the land of the former Athens airport, the Athens International airport, the Greek gas utility company, and the Greek railway maintenance company] be financially closed by the end of the year, additional proceeds of over €1.5 billion are expected in the second half of 2018, which would give a cumulative yield of some €4.5 billion since the start of the ESM programme", the report mentions.
>
> (*I Kathimerini*, 20.06.2018)

With expressions like "the report says", or "[the report] mentions the risks the Greek economy may face", agency is attributed to the report, while its authors – and the political and other actors who are involved in the bailout-related decisions, implementation, and their evaluation – are completely absent. Also, in the last part of the article a hypothesis is presented regarding the outcome of ongoing privatisations, using a series of data for support, while there is no information or estimation on what may happen should these privatisations be further delayed or never completed. Still, these predictions are given the status of fact and not speculation, since they are being reported by an official, objective document and not by political or other actors – who are totally invisible anyway.

The signifying practice of reifying the economy and the markets helps to treat entities such as the economy, the banking system, or society, as unified and unitary, and not as products of social and political tensions, conflict and struggle. Similarly, through reification, the bailout-related policies are legitimated as orchestrated and operated by distant, independent, and uncontrollable centres of power. At the same time, this practice protects the involved actors' positions of authority, as it helps to dissociate the actors and the institutions they represent, from the political decisions and their implementation, preventing them from being held accountable. The reification of economic activity, argues Gaye Tuchman (1978a, 214), reaffirms the status quo, by on the one hand legitimating the politicians' and the governments' powerlessness to battle the forces of the economy (in case they fail), and on the other, legitimating their authority in case their actions are seen as successful. At the level of journalistic practice, reification allows journalists to distance themselves from the sources of power that they report on – and who happen to be among their privileged sources of information.

Discourse of naturalisation

Naturalisation, as already explained, relates to the discursive practices of presenting information and ideas as common-sense knowledge, or as events created by external, natural forces. Naturalisation implies that there is "an immutable 'natural order of things' [. . .] and presents a context wherein unavoidable events might lead to a particular outcome" (Reshef and Keim

2014, 99). Through the constituents of naturalisation – symbolic annihilation, mystification, and moralisation – information, opinions, and positions regarding the economic crisis are treated "as the way thigs are" (Tuchman 1978a, 196), as inescapable reality to be taken for granted.

Symbolic annihilation – omission, trivialisation, condemnation

The mechanisms of omission, condemnation, and trivialisation constitute what has been described by Tuchman as symbolic annihilation (1978b, 17). These signifying practices involve processes of exclusion or misrepresentation of social groups in the news, which can lead to these groups' symbolic neutralisation and disappearance.

In our study, these practices are often observed in the sources' efforts to legitimate their positions and delegitimate those of other actors. For example, it is common that EU-related actors that appear as sources in the bailout-related news attempt to condemn the Greek side for its non-compliance or unwillingness to abide by what has been agreed and to work towards solutions. In this process, the focus is on ungrateful or non-compliant Greece, while vital information on the terms of the bailouts, the negotiations, and the measures implemented – which are usually particularly harsh – are either omitted or trivialised as information of minor importance.

Through the **omission** of important information for the comprehension of an issue, a particular version of reality is constructed that favours specific interpretations and deprivileges some others. The construction of reality through omission creates a discursive environment that excludes alternative or multiple interpretations of social phenomena and promotes rather unitary constructions of reality. The following example of omission comes from the period after the implementation of the second bailout agreement, which did not manage to lead to economic recovery and contributed to political turmoil due to the inability to form a government in Greece. In this excerpt, vital information for the comprehension of the topic discussed is absent, and at the same time, predictions and speculations constructed around very selective components of the issue, are presented as facts:

> [Fitch] avoids, however, to make clear what the consequences of Greece leaving will be for the Eurozone, as [the rating agency] describes them as "uncertain" and stresses that they will depend on the way the exit is materialised and on the reaction of Europe. It just emphasises that it will give a negative review to all the other Eurozone countries' rates, if Greece abandons the Eurozone either because of the current political crisis, or later if its economy is not stabilised.
>
> (*I Kathimerini*, 12.05.2012)

In this example, while specific information on the repercussions that a potential Grexit would have for the Eurozone is lacking, in the absence of information a certainty is created regarding the rating agency's decision to give negative reviews to all the Eurozone countries' rates, in the case of a Grexit. Through this warning, which exerts pressure against a potential Grexit, Fitch, exercising its authority of expertise, rationalises and legitimates its decision through a projection into the future, without providing any further information.

In the following example, the terms that follow Greece's exodus from the third Memorandum are evaluated positively and are euphemised as "relief instruments", while the conditions that Greece has to abide by are largely downplayed and omitted:

> Less or no problematic at all are the rest of the relief instruments for Greece. The return of the central banks' profits from the Greek bonds will be linked to the condition that the Greek government does not deviate from the reform path and meets the targets for primary surpluses. At the same time, Greece will have a safety cushion in order to have liquidity, if necessary, for up to two years, without issuing bonds.
>
> (*Ta Nea*, 21b.06.2018)

In this example, there is no information on what "the targets for primary surpluses" are (which are harsh and very difficult to abide by); similarly, the "reform path" from which Greece cannot deviate is a euphemism for neoliberal measures related to further pension cuts and privatisations.

Still, it should be mentioned that in the previous paragraph of the same article, there are some references to the negotiation regarding the extension of the period within which Greece has to pay off the €130.9 bn of loans given through the second Memorandum. The decision to reject the proposal for an additional 15-year extension is legitimated with an argument that is not substantiated by any information:

> The original proposal for another 15-year extension has been withdrawn after Germany's resistance, which is not alone in this issue, says [German newspaper] "Handelsblatt", citing European diplomatic sources. "There is a limit to extension, so that the debt can be paid back in one generation", explained to "*Ta Nea*" Gunther Krichbaum, chair of the Committee on European Union Affairs in Bundestag. "From then on it is essentially a debt write-off".

The rejection of the proposal for an (additional) extension is thus legitimated by the journalist, who does not scrutinise the German politician's view (e.g., by investigating whether other countries did repay their debts in periods longer than that of "one generation"), and instead takes it at face value, treating it as a truth statement and a natural fact, and not as an opinion or political decision.

When it is not omitted, important information regarding the terms of the bailout agreements, their implementation, and their implications for people's lives (as they involve harsh measures) can be **trivialised** or downplayed as of minor importance. The strategies of treating as procedural or bureaucratic, critical phases of the negotiations between the Greek side and the lenders, which are frequently encountered in the EU-related actors' public discourse, fall within this logic. Similarly, in an effort to ease concerns stemming from the possibility of Greece's exit from the Eurozone, EU-related actors would downplay or trivialise its repercussions, or treat it as a procedural issue and not as an issue of major importance that would affect a lot of sectors of social and economic activity and thus peoples' lives. For example, during the time that the Troika was putting pressure to the Syriza government to comply with the previously agreed terms, the president of ECB, Mario Draghi, was explaining that it is "business as usual" to develop Grexit scenarios, trivialising this possibility: "Asked about whether the ECB is examining scenarios of Greece leaving the euro, he [Draghi] said that analysts and bank executives analyse all risks, because this is their job, it is a normal practice" (*I Kathimerini*, 24.03.2015).

Also, as both newspapers studied do not support the Syriza government, they tend to trivialise, through the selection and positioning of their sources, any measures that are announced by the government to ease economic pressure as being populist, unrealistic, or of low significance – thus suggesting that the measures will not be of much help to those who have suffered from the government's policies so far. In the following example, the journalist is directly critiquing the government and the governmental sources used for this article as untrustworthy, through an ironic and moralising tone. At the same time, the journalist trivialises and downplays the importance of the efforts to ease the economic pressure on the Greek people:

> In the government, after the festivities for having solved the big issues, they are planning to turn to the daily issues. [. . .] The Prime Minister's close team intends to launch specific government interventions that will improve, as they say, citizens' daily lives. [. . .] At the same time, in order to strengthen their lost left profile, they seem to be investing a lot in cancelling the pre-voted reductions in pensions and tax-free allowances. What if the latter have been decided? [. . .] Reading, therefore, between the lines, someone could see in the governmental leaks a return to the pre-crisis habits. To the era of promises.
>
> (*Ta Nea*, 25.06.2018)

Trivialisation also relates to a common journalistic practice that bears significant implications for the content of the produced news. After initially having spent some time providing the basic information on an issue, journalists tend to treat previously mentioned information as common knowledge, and present any relevant new information by building on the earlier reported news, which is briefly brought up (if brought up at all), in order to focus on the new development. This discursive practice of treating information that is important for the comprehension of an issue as everyday, common knowledge, or less important is related not only to the routines of news production but also to conscious efforts by news sources and journalists to offer an interpretative framework for both new and old information. The ideological implications of this process, which "creates an order of (un)importance of the information presented, sketching a map of evaluative relations" (Doudaki 2018, 150), is that previously introduced information acquires the status of (unquestioned) naturalised knowledge.

As already mentioned, EU actors frequently attempt to legitimate their position of authority against Greece by accusing it of being untrustworthy. In the following example, an EU official blames the newly elected government of Syriza of improper (and unethical) handling of the negotiations:

> A European official, wishing to describe the climate, said to "K" that any new government starts with "zero" trust and has to earn it, but the handling by the new Greek government, mainly with the leaks that took place the past weeks, put the partners' confidence "in minus", as he characteristically says.
>
> (*I Kathimerini*, 22.02.2015)

Following this line of (moralistic) reasoning, the EU member states that are in economic difficulty are by definition untrustworthy until proven reliable; this is not, of course, the case with the EU officials and institutions, whose credentials are taken for granted. In this and in similar examples, the implementation of fragmentation and differentiation strategies (Thompson 1990, 65) help to create a polarising environment of opposing groups and enemies that need to be annihilated, often through a moralising discourse. Fragmentation functions by isolating the groups or individuals "that might be orientating forces of potential opposition towards a target which is projected as evil, harmful or threatening" (ibid.), while differentiation functions through "emphasizing the distinctions, differences and divisions between individuals and groups, the characteristics which disunite them and prevent them from constituting an effective challenge to existing relations or an effective participant in the exercise of power" (ibid.). Also, in cases where fragmentation and differentiation are not sufficient for the clear construction of the enemy, the "expurgation of the other" is put into effect. This strategy involves the representation of an adversary "which is portrayed as evil, harmful or threatening and which individuals are called upon collectively to resist or expurgate" (ibid.).

In the following example, the leader of the conservative opposition party, Kyriakos Mitsotakis, is critiquing the government and trying to downplay the "exodus" from the third Memorandum, which had been confirmed by the EU partners a few days previously. Using the strategy of displacement – in which one object, individual, or term "is used to refer to another, and thereby the positive or negative connotations of the term are transferred to the other object or individual" (Thompson 1990, 62) – Mitsotakis is labelling the exodus agreement as a "fourth Memorandum", focussing on the harsh terms that the agreement entails. He then later, using highly moralising language, accuses the Syriza–ANEL coalition government in general, and Prime Minister Alexis Tsipras in particular, of cynicism and dishonesty, in an attempt to present Tsipras as harmful for the country:

> In a sharp tone, he [Mr. Mitsotakis] accuses Mr. Tsipras of "cynicism", as the latter does not talk about the imminent new cuts that are coming, while he calls him "presumptuous and arrogant", "offending the intelligence of the Greek people". "We will not let SYRIZANEL's unscrupulous propaganda hide their disastrous choices with fiestas and new lies" [Mr. Mitsotakis argued and added that the Prime Minister] "will apologise for all the suffering he has brought to the citizens, but also for the shackles he agreed to, for the country's future."
>
> (*I Kathimerini*, 23.06.2018)

In the following example, the journalist presents what the real situation will be for the Greek economy after the end of the third Memorandum, in a critical and demeaning tone. The journalist interprets (not simply presents) the sources' (representatives of the lenders) statements, and critiques the government for being dishonest or unrealistic when it argues that the country will leave the Memoranda behind:

> Representatives of the lenders deliver a strict message to Athens for the next day, insisting on the continuation of reforms and making clear at the same time that supervision will be tighter. The Greek economy will be found in a tunnel of tight surveillance for many years, right after the end of the third programme, with lenders announcing quarterly evaluations, deconstructing the government's narrative of a "clean exit" from the Memoranda, on 20 August.
>
> (*Ta Nea*, 15.06.2018)

Symbolic annihilation and its constituents – omission, trivialisation, and condemnation – are used by elite actors in the news in their attempts to legitimate their positions and maintain their authority by discrediting and undermining those of their opponents. Also, bailout-related policies and measures are symbolically annihilated as either harmful or inefficient by the opposition, while their implications are downplayed as unimportant and trivial by the Troika or the Greek governments. Symbolic annihilation is used as both a defensive strategy, when the actors' own positions are attacked or questioned, and as an offensive strategy in unequal power relations, when the actors attempt to either consolidate or strengthen their power positions (e.g. Troika actors) or change the power balance to their benefit (e.g. the Greek side). As a journalistic practice, symbolic annihilation allows journalists to maintain their authority as objective news professionals while they actively intervene in the interpretation of the information they present. The way to maintain their authority is through the selection and management of sources that appear in their news stories, since the sources – and not the journalists – are presented as the carriers of information and its suggested interpretations.

Mystification

When information about the components and dimensions of the economic crisis in Greece is not completely omitted or trivialised, it may be mystified. Mystification concerns the creation of a blurred or obscured discursive environment where insinuations and half-explained (or half-implied) information and facts help to support and legitimate actions, policies, and decisions without the involved actors having to fully explain and account for them (Doudaki 2018, 151). In that sense, mystification is served also by omission, given that omitted pieces of information support the creation of the mystified environment.

Mystification can entail blackboxing. "Blackboxing" refers to the concealment, or coverage from view or scrutiny, of processes and practices pertinent to the production of knowledge. Science philosopher Bruno Latour was among the first to bring the term in the broad field of social sciences. As he explained, "[t]he word black box is used by cyberneticians whenever a piece of machinery or a set of commands is too complex. In its place they draw a little box about which they need to know nothing but its input and output" (1987, 2–3). Based on this, blackboxing relates to the ways in which scientific and technical work is made invisible: "When a machine runs efficiently, when a matter of fact is settled, one need focus only on its inputs and outputs and not on its internal complexity. Thus, paradoxically, the more science and technology succeed, the more opaque and obscure they become" (Latour 1999, 304). Used more broadly, the term black box "describes accepted and agreed pieces of knowledge. A black-box is often part of a more complicated system that is so unquestioned and stable that it can be ignored within that system" (Rice 2011, 33).

Blackboxing can be part of mystification, as it hides the internal complexity of the processes that lead to certain outcomes regarding, in our case, the handling of the economic crisis. A lot of the political processes that involved negotiations and decision-making in relation to the bailout agreements were actually blackboxed. Still, mystification as it is used in our analysis, is broader than blackboxing, as it also describes situations and practices of semi-transparency or blurriness, given that the political actors are expected or called upon to provide some information about the processes, interactions, and negotiations that they are involved in, on the premise of accountability that democracy entails.

In the following example, Geogre Katroungalos, the Syriza government Minister of Labour, attempts to legitimate the government's policy regarding the drastic labour reforms that were dictated by the then-recently approved third Memorandum, arguing that the government has "alternative" plans. However, no precise information is given, and it never becomes clear what the reform will entail. A lot is left unexplained and a lot more is being implied. Through this vagueness the message is communicated that the government, which had been forced to sign the Memorandum, still has alternatives:

> Although the Memorandum that was voted by the government last week includes a range of measures, with pension cuts, contribution increases, and the target, within 2016, that all pension funds come under one, single structure, [. . .] the new Minister of Labour said yesterday that he will pursue the implementation of another, different reform. The basic principles of this "alternative" reform have been approved by the Prime Minister. [. . .] The Minister of Labour did not want to show his cards in relation to the actual content of the reform, and when asked about the future of the supplementary pensions and the implementation of the zero-deficit clause, he hinted that with his proposal, the matter may be overcome.
>
> (*I Kathimerini*, 20.08.2015)

In this article, in which "the implementation of another, different reform" is blackboxed, the journalist is taking some distance from the Minister's position by exposing the arbitrary logics created through mystification. The journalist is framing the Minister's arguments in such a way that it becomes clear that those are unfounded or not sufficiently legitimated. It is worth mentioning that when the newspapers studied distance themselves from the positions and policies of the institutional sources that appear in the articles analysed, they normally do not rebuke the authority of the latter explicitly or fundamentally; they rather indirectly or mildly raise doubts or discredit the arguments and positions of these sources through symbolic annihilation and other signifying practices. Still, there are some exceptions to this norm, more frequently encountered in *Ta Nea* during the period of research that covers the events around the third Memorandum and the completion of its terms.

Through the strategy of dissimulation – which allows for the representation of events, processes, and power struggles – "in a way which deflects attention from or glosses over existing relations or processes" (Thompson 1990, 62), news about the economic crisis and the bailout agreements tends to be presented in a decontextualised and concealed or obscured fashion. Not rarely, mystification is ahistorical. Through eternalisation, "social-historical phenomena are deprived of their historical character by being portrayed as permanent, unchanging and ever-recurring" (ibid., 66). Eternalising the contingent helps to normalise contested political decisions and actions. In these cases, intention and speculation are framed as event, action, or reality, and are often taken out of their temporal or political context.

In the following example of mystification, activated through blackboxing, EU Commissioner Pierre Moscovici's statement is particularly vague, disconnected from any temporal, structural, or other dimension:

> EU Commissioner Pierre Moscovici said yesterday that "the Finance Ministers and the European Commission must definitely decide on Thursday on a package of important relief measures for the Greek debt", while in his answer to the member of the European Parliament, Nikos Chountis, he stresses that there will be measures for the debt with future policy commitments.
>
> (*Ta Nea*, 19.06.2018)

No concrete information is provided on what the measures for the alleviation of Greek debt will entail in the post-Memorandum era; when they will be agreed upon and implemented; or which structures, institutions, and actors will decide on and be involved in the measures' implementation. The matter is blackboxed, pushed to the indefinite future.

Signification practices of mystification often involve euphemisations in which, "actions, institutions or social relations are described or redescribed in terms which elicit a positive valuation" (Thompson 1990, 62) (e.g. in the earlier excerpt, "relief measures for the Greek debt"). In the following example, the deal regarding the exodus of Greece from the third Memorandum is positively signified as the guarantee of Greece's continuation "on the road to fiscal stability and reforms":

> The same sources believe that the overall solution will be trustworthy for the markets, for the lenders who want to have the necessary safeguards that Greece will continue on the road to fiscal stability and reforms, but it will also be beneficial for Greece and its citizens.
> (*Ta Nea*, 20a.06.2018).

The readers are given a vague promise by anonymous sources that the deal "will be beneficial for Greece and its citizens" without further explanation or more information on how this will be guaranteed.

Insinuations, promises, vagueness, and concealment are put into use for the creation of a mystified environment that helps the involved actors legitimate the bailout agreements and their measures. Through mystification, the elite actors who appear as sources in the news attempt to create an opaque discursive environment that will allow them to maintain their authority positions, either by blackboxing parts of the processes and the internal complexities of these processes that lead to certain decisions, or by postponing for the future decisions regarding (harsh) measures and their implications. Mystification helps also journalists to protect their authority by transferring to their sources the responsibility for accountability that journalists have to their audiences. They leave it up to the sources to sufficiently explain (or not explain) the dimensions and outcomes of the crisis-related events.

Moralisation

"Moralisation broadly refers to the use of language that is connected to, or evokes, moral codes and values to describe and explain a situation or phenomenon" (Doudaki 2018, 152). Focussing on the entanglement of moralisation and naturalisation, Van Leeuwen approaches naturalisation as a specific form of moral evaluation, "which in fact denies morality and replaces moral and cultural orders with the 'natural order'. Morality and nature become entangled" (2007, 99).

Moralisation is easy to communicate, as it is recognised on the basis of one's "commonsense cultural knowledge" (Reshef and Keim 2014, 195). As it is "expressive of the deep bonds that hold us together" (ibid.), it is not necessary to explain "an action's moral significance" (ibid.) to the audience. A moralising language, often articulated around words, phrases, and images of good, evil, virtue, and evaluative adjectives and phrases – it's normal, it's natural, it's healthy, etc. – functions as "the tip of a submerged iceberg of moral values [which] trigger a moral concept, but are detached from the system of interpretation from which they derive" (Van Leeuwen 2007, 97, 2018, 147). Hence, in order to understand the moral status of such ethical assessments, it is important to look into the opaque tissue of history and culture "by tracing them back to the moral discourses that underlie them, and by undoing the 'genesis amnesia' (Bourdieu 1979, 79) that allows us to treat such moral evaluations as commonsense values that have always existed" (Van Leeuwen 2007, 98, 2018, 148).

Previous research has shown that moralising discourse is often used in news coverage about crime, "deviant" behaviour, marginal social groups, and conflict (e.g., Hall et al. 1978; Cohen 2011; Critcher 2003; Hammond 2000; Denham 2008). Also, political decisions and actions are often legitimated or delegitimated by the actors involved and by news media, resorting to cultural and ethical norms and values, relating political action "to the prevalent moral order of society" (Van Dijk 1998, 256).

In our study, fairness, trust, truth, and morality – as well as their opposites –, are often evoked to argue in favour of or against the Memoranda and their implications. The bailout measures and policies are often described as fair or unfair, while austerity is often described as cruel or unjust to the Greek people. Also, the Troika and the Greek governments' actors regularly accuse each other of being misleading or untrustworthy. Similarly, within the Greek political system the opposition often accuses the government of "not keeping its promises", and of "lying to the Greek people". Moralisation quite efficiently supports critique and blame, as it transfers to the critique the entire value system that it relates to, without having to unpack it. This is one of the reasons why moralisation can be a powerful legitimation strategy: "[I]t 'attacks' the innermost core of human existence – its value system" (Reshef and Keim 2014, 119).

For example, when the Syriza government was negotiating with the Troika on the terms of the programme that would follow the second Memorandum, and as the Troika partners became less willing to compromise and put more pressure to the Greek side, Prime Minister Alexis Tsipras is quoted as saying that ECB President Mario Draghi, "took a 'politically and ethically unorthodox' decision to limit the liquidity of the state". Similarly, later on:

> Mr. Varoufakis confirmed yesterday the allegation of Mr. Tsipras [that he was misled by the President of Eurogroup, Jeroen Dijsselbloem], saying that "there was no commitment to the word of honour". We, he said, went with the feeling that a deal is a deal. That when we shake hands for "a" and not for "b", this means "a" and not "b".
>
> (*Ta Nea*, 29.04.2015)

This moralising argument about the need to commit to the word of honour reflects the communicative approach by the Syriza government in its first stage of negotiations with the Troika, which was systematically adopted by the Greek Minister of Finance, Yanis Varoufakis, who led the negotiations at the time.

The discussion on "confidence", "trust", "lack of trust", and "regaining trust" is central during the negotiations regarding the terms of the Memoranda. Greece is generally framed as untrustworthy by the EU partners, and its compliance with the creditors' expectations will restore, or build, its trustworthiness: "For his part, the member of the board of ECB, Christian Noyer, stressed that the other Eurozone countries want Greece to get into a 'clear reform path' and regain its trust with a convincing reform programme" (*I Kathimerini*, 24.03.2015).

The values of solidarity are also often called upon, to legitimate both support and discipline. The following example employs the strategy of "unification", embracing groups and individuals "in a collective identity, irrespective of the differences and divisions that may separate them" (Thompson 1990, 64). In a complementary fashion, after groups and individuals are unified in one identify, they are further infused the collective identity's unifying values. In this example, the leader of ESM describes Europe as one family, with Greece being one of its members:

> Most importantly, however, Mr. Regling sent the message that the ESM [European Stability Mechanism] – and by extension the European partners – "will not abandon Greece" once the programme is over. If necessary, "Europe is ready to help in the long run", he mentioned, adding that "solidarity does not end in August" [. . . .]. In other words, as explained by a source of the institutions [Troika] [. . .] the solution regarding the debt decided by the Eurogroup may not be that bold, but this should not be a cause for concern, because Europe will take care of Greece, if necessary, since it is a member of the family.
>
> (*I Kathimerini*, 15.06.2018)

A similar moralised discourse of punishment and reward is frequently used:

> In other words, they decided that after the end of the three Memoranda, Greece will continue to be under "enhanced supervision", and if it respects the agreements with its lenders, it will be rewarded, otherwise it will be penalised. It will be rewarded with approximately one billion euro a year for the next four years if its economic policies are positively

assessed by Brussels and will be in danger of re-enacting a Memorandum if its economic policies are evaluated negatively.

(*Ta Nea*, 20b.06.2018)

Both the Greek government and the opposition regularly employ a populist rhetoric in regard to either the protection or destruction of the Greek people's future, or to the Greek people's sacrifices that are either bearing fruit or are in vain. For example, the Greek Prime Minister refers to the imminent finalisation of the third Memorandum, arguing that

> "We are very close to the moment when the years-long hard sacrifices on the part of the Greek people, will bear fruit" [. . .] adding that he expects today "a decision to regulate the Greek debt that will mark the end of the eight-year adventure for Greece".
>
> (*Ta Nea*, 21a.06.2018)

Patriotism is also called upon. Here, it is connected to trust in the Greek banking system, by the leader of the socialist party PASOK during the period of the double 2012 elections: "'And the Greek depositors must understand that it is important to help our country, patriotically trusting the Greek banking system, guaranteed through a series of decisions by the Eurozone', said Mr. Venizelos" (*Ta Nea*, 12.06.2012). Also, analogies and comparisons (positive and negative), seem to have a moralising capacity (Van Leeuwen 2007, 99–100). For this purpose, historical events from either the heroic or disastrous past are recalled, to explain the degree of a phenomenon or legitimate certain actions. For example, the Tsipras government's initially strong negative reaction to the creditors' terms was described by the opposition as suicidal and was compared to specific historical events of great national disaster. The condensed symbolic and emotional load of these events (of suffering and destruction, but also in other cases, of heroism, resistance, etc.) is transferred to the new event or phenomenon with which they are related, without having to engage in lengthy analyses, which serves the journalistic need for economy in writing (Doudaki 2018, 154).

The elite actors who appear in the bailout-related news as sources engage heavily in moralisation. Moralisation can have strong emotional effects, helping these actors to legitimate positions and decisions regarding the crisis and its handling. Moralisation also enhances the efficiency of all the other legitimation mechanisms. Even clearly rationalised arguments and decisions can be strengthened when dressed in moral armour, which increases the chances that they "have positive moral connotations and receive popular support as the right things to do" (Reshef and Keim 2014, 99). Especially when it comes to the harsh measures taken to tackle the crisis, the argument of necessity or of future problem-solving may not suffice, and a clear justification based on acceptable by the public ethical standards, can elevate these policies to the level of moral rectitude. From the perspective of journalistic practice, moralisation helps journalists to normalise as common-sensical value-laden information and opinions, presenting them as natural, therefore neutral and objective information.

Notes

1 The date 25a.06.2018 signifies that this is the first of several articles published in the same date (25 June) by the same newspaper, which are used here as examples of the analysis.

2 Yanis Varoufakis was Minister of Finance from January 2015 until early July 2015. He led the negotiations with Greece's creditors during the first months of the Syriza–ANEL government, but he not not manage to reach an agreement with the Troika. Following the 2015 Greek bailout referendum on 5 July, and the rejection of the Troika bailout terms by the majority of Greeks, there was disagreement with Prime Minister Alexis Tsipras on the government's line in the post-referendum period, which led to Varoufakis's resignation as Minister of Finance (Varoufakis 2015).

3 Before the elections that brought Syriza to power.

4 The concept of reification was originally developed by Karl Marx (see, e.g. 1976) and it has been linked with Marxist thought, though not exclusively. Petrović (1983, 411) defines reification as:

> The act (or result of the act) of transforming human properties, relations and actions into properties, relations and actions of man-produced things which have become independent (and which are imagined as originally independent) of man and govern his life.

For the diverse uses of, and approaches to, reification, see e.g. the work of Marxist philosopher György Lukács (2000), the Frankfurt School scholars Horkheimer and Adorno (2002), and French philosopher Louis Althusser's (2005) critique of the term.

References

Althusser, Louis. 2005. *For Marx*. Translated by Ben Brewster. London: Verso.

Berger, Peter L., and Thomas Luckmann. 1967. *The Social Construction of Reality*. London: Penguin Books.

Bourdieu, Pierre. 1979. *Outline of a Theory of Practice*. Translated by Richard Nice. Cambridge: Cambridge University Press.

Cohen, Stanley. 2011. *Folk Devils and Moral Panics*. London: Routledge.

Critcher, Chas. 2003. *Moral Panics and the Media*. Buckingham: Open University Press.

Denham, Bryan E. 2008. "Folk Devils, News Icons and the Construction of Moral Panics: Heroin Chic and the Amplification of Drug Threats in Contemporary Society." *Journalism Studies* 9 (6): 945–61.

Doudaki, Vaia. 2015. "Legitimation Mechanisms in the Bailout Discourse." *Javnost: The Public* 22 (1): 1–17.

Doudaki, Vaia. 2018. "Discourses of Legitimation in the News: The Case of the Cypriot Bailout." In *Cyprus and Its Conflicts: Representations, Materialities and Cultures*, edited by Vaia Doudaki and Nico Carpentier, 142–62. New York: Berghahn Books.

Goddard, Peter. 1998. "Press Rhetoric and Economic News: A Case Study." In *The Economy, Media and Public Knowledge*, edited by Neil T. Gavin, 71–89. London: Leicester University Press.

Hall, Stuart, Chas Critcher, Tony Jefferson, John Clarke, and Brian Roberts. 1978. *Policing the Crisis: Mugging, the State, and Law and Order*. New York: Palgrave Macmillan.

Hammond, Philip. 2000. "'Good Versus Evil' after the Cold War: Kosovo and the Moralisation of War Reporting." *Javnost: The Public* 7 (3): 19–37.

Horkheimer, Max, and Theodor W. Adorno. 2002. *Dialectic of Enlightenment*. Translated by Edmund Jephcott. Stanford, CA: Stanford University Press.

Kelly, Peter. 2000. "Youth as an Artefact of Expertise: Problematizing the Practice of Youth Studies in an Age of Uncertainty." *Journal of Youth Studies* 3 (3): 301–15.

Latour, Bruno. 1987. *Science in Action*. Cambridge, MA: Harvard University Press.

Latour, Bruno. 1999. *Pandora's Hope: Essays on the Reality of Science Studies*. Cambridge, MA: Harvard University Press.

Lukács, György. 2000. *History and Class Consciousness: Studies in Marxist Dialectics*. Cambridge, MA: The MIT Press.

Marx, Karl. 1976. *Capital: A Critique of Political Economy*. London: Penguin Books.

Petrović, Gajo. 1983. "Reification." In *A Dictionary of Marxist Thought*, edited by Tom Bottomore, Laurence Harris, V.G. Kiernan, and Ralph Miliband, 411–13. Cambridge, MA: Harvard University Press. www.marxists.org/archive/petrovic/1965/reification.htm.

Porter, Theodore M. 1995. *Trust in Numbers: The Pursuit of Objectivity in Science and Public Life*. Princeton, NJ: Princeton University Press.

Reshef, Yonatan, and Charles Keim. 2014. *Bad Time Stories: Government-Union Conflicts and the Rhetoric of Legitimation Strategies*. Toronto: University of Toronto Press.

Rice, Louis. 2011. "Black-Boxing Sustainability." *Journal of Sustainable Development* 4 (4): 32–7.

Rose, Nikolas. 1990. *Governing the Soul*. London: Routledge.

Rose, Nikolas, and Peter Miller. 1992. "Political Power Beyond the State: Problematics of Government." *British Journal of Sociology* 43 (2): 173–205.

Smith, Marc C. 1994. *Social Science in the Crucible: The American Debate over Objectivity and Purpose, 1918–1941*. Durham, NC: Duke University Press.

Thompson, John B. 1990. *Ideology and Modern Culture: Critical Social Theory in the Era of Mass Communication.* Cambridge: Polity Press.

Tuchman, Gaye. 1978a. *Making News: A Study in the Construction of Reality.* New York: Free Press.

Tuchman, Gaye. 1978b. "Introduction: The Symbolic Annihilation of Women by the Mass Media." In *Hearth and Home: Images of Women in the Mass Media*, edited by Gaye Tuchman, Arlene Kaplan Daniels, and James Benet, 3–38. New York: Oxford University Press.

Van Dijk, Teun A. 1998. *Ideology: A Multidisciplinary Approach.* London: Sage.

Van Leeuwen, Theo. 2007. "Legitimation in Discourse and Communication." *Discourse & Communication* 1 (1): 91–112.

Van Leeuwen, Theo. 2018. "Moral Evaluation in Critical Discourse Analysis." *Critical Discourse Studies* 15 (2): 140–53.

Varoufakis, Yanis. 2015. "Minister No More!." 6 July. www.yanisvaroufakis.eu/2015/07/06/minister-no-more/.

Concluding reflections

Vaia Doudaki

This study explored the discursive struggles over legitimation of decisions, policies, and authority positions of actors related to the economic crisis in Greece, by studying news articles published in two leading Greek newspapers. The analysis identified two overarching discourses of legitimation – objectivation and naturalisation – that the protagonists of the crisis engage with, in order to support their positions and discredit those of their opponents.

The study focussed on the investigation of the role of news sources, a role which is conducive to the legitimation of not only political and other elite actors' authority, but also of journalists themselves. The dominance of specific types of sources in the news, mainly from the political establishment, is indicative of who the newspapers treat not only as information providers but also as sources of power. These sources, for their part, validate through their presence in the news the journalists' jurisdiction over the collection and dissemination of information on issues of general concern for societies, confirming journalists' role and status. As the analysis showed, journalists and their sources enhance each other's legitimacy, in a process of mutual authority confirmation.

The two discourses

As became clear through the analysis, the discourses of objectivation and naturalisation function in such a way as to establish and confirm the status of the actors who are involved in the crisis, to legitimate the bailout-related policies and their accompanying ideologies, and to reconfirm journalistic jurisdiction.

Objectivation – constructed through expertise, quantification, and reification – allows for the presentation of information and ideas as "real", "neutral" facts, as non-ideological and value-free. The presence of experts in the news stories allows journalists to demonstrate that journalism as a profession uses methods of news gathering found in the sciences, resorting to expert knowledge for the presentation and explanation of complex issues, such as the ones pertinent to the economic crisis and its handling. The use of expert sources in bailout-related news stories is highly instrumental. Market and economy connoisseurs appear in the news articles studied in order to (usually) offer support to the bailout deals and their terms. Through the authority of expertise, speculations and predictions are elevated to the status of objective facticity, presented within suggested frameworks of meaning by the knowledgeable voices of seemingly detached outsiders, which non-experts (i.e. the public) cannot easily contest.

Also, through the use of numbers and data, the news stories attain the character of objectivity and help journalists to maintain their authority positions as detached professionals. Still, as shown by the analysis, quantification can turn data into "tools of persuasion" (Goddard 1998, 87). Data are used strategically as hard facts, difficult to contest, thus the events they are connected to, and the crisis reality that is constructed with their help, are also hard to contest. Additionally, as the legitimation mechanisms do not work in isolation but rather in combination (Reshef and Keim 2014, 18), the combined presence of quantification and expertise, delivering data through expert sources, enhances their effectiveness.

Moreover, through reification – a mechanism through which the products of human activity gain agency, while humans themselves lose agency – the actors related to the crisis are dissociated from the agreed-upon and implemented policies, and thus their status can be protected: It is the markets, seen as all-powerful, uncontrollable forces, that exert pressure for the implementation of harsh neoliberal policies; it is the Memoranda (bailout agreements), the budgets, the conformity reports, etc., that force the implementation of the agreed-upon measures. Furthermore, the reification of the economy and its mechanisms allows for its de-politisation, thereby concealing the ideological foundations on which the economic system is based. Journalists' authority as objective professionals is also protected through reification, since they appear to be neutrally reporting on the reified phenomena of the crisis, distancing themselves from the ideological positions that support the crisis policies.

Naturalisation, the second main discourse of legitimation, functions at the level of journalistic practice in ways that support – through symbolic annihilation, mystification, and moralisation – the "news as story" logic, while still protecting the ideal of the objective narrative, and thus the authority of journalists as the legitimate storytellers of events of current affairs. Naturalisation legitimates the role of journalists as the ones who possess the skills and the jurisdiction to tell society what is important for it to know. In the case of the economic crisis in Greece, journalists function as the authoritative storytellers of the crisis, by deciding what is of relevance for the Greek public to know and how the story of the crisis should be reconstructed, and by mediating between the main decision-makers and the Greek public in regard to the issues at stake over the crisis. At the same time, naturalisation helps to legitimate the hegemonic discourses around the crisis and to confirm the involved actors' status positions. This is achieved by providing the interpretative framework with which to understand the constituents of the crisis and the values with which to legitimate these discourses and the implemented policies, as well as by enabling the neutralisation of the accompanying ideologies.

Through omission, trivialisation, and condemnation, status positions and policies regarding the crisis are symbolically annihilated as unimportant, inefficient, or harmful, by news sources and journalists alike. Symbolic annihilation is also used by the Greek governments or the Troika actors to delegitimate the critique on the repercussions of the implemented policies, by treating these consequences as trivial or of lesser importance, in comparison to the long-term gains for the Greek economy. At the level of journalistic practice, symbolic annihilation allows journalists to bring value-laden perspectives to the issues they report on, and to maintain their authority positions as objective professionals, since it is their sources and not themselves who articulate these value judgements.

Mystification assists in the creation of an obscure discursive environment, concerning the economic crisis and its treatment, through half-explained information, insinuation, and blackboxing. By concealing parts of the processes and practices that relate to the economic system and its pathogenies, and by hiding the involvement of specific actors in these processes, mystification helps these actors maintain or re-establish their authority. Also, journalists can protect their status, as responsibility for providing thorough explanations about the constituents of the crisis (and any failure to do so) is fully assigned to their sources.

The discursive practice of moralisation – which transfers the moral values associated with events or people to other actions, policies, and actors – helps to cover decisions and policies with a blanket of values, and through this practice to rationalise them with the "self-evident" qualities that these values bring along. Moralisation helps to divert the discussion about the economic crisis, as it obscures the importance of rational argumentation in regard to the crisis reality, by focussing on value assessments presented in the place of arguments and facts. This practice helps journalists to present ethically, emotionally, or ideologically charged opinions and ideas as neutral information by treating them as natural and common-sense.

It may appear that the strategies of objectivation serve (exclusively) the "news as fact" logic while naturalisation serves the "news as story" logic.

However this distinction is more of an analytical nature and thus partly artificial, as objectivation and naturalisation are neither mutually exclusive nor separate. On the contrary, they function as two sides of a coin, enhancing each other's efficiency.

The media and the broader environment

These discourses are articulated in specific contexts and are presented in specific media by journalists working in these media. Thus a reflection on the role of the media studied and of their broader environment is highly relevant. The two newspapers, *I Kathimerini* and *Ta Nea*, supported the three Memoranda and their logics of implementation throughout the 2010–2018 period, and attempted to use their coverage to legitimate the pro-Memoranda policies and discourses (see e.g. Doudaki et al. 2016; Doudaki 2015). Occasionally they may have been critical towards the Troika for being too harsh against Greece, but this stance concerned mainly the first two Memoranda, and in particular the phases of negotiation between Greece and the Troika regarding the terms of the bailouts. Once the agreements were reached, they supported them clearly and consistently as the only way out of Greece's economic deadlock (and also as an opportunity to "cure" Greece's pathogenies – see, e.g. Mylonas 2014).

Following this logic, the two newspapers undertook a monitorial role[1] in their news coverage of the economic crisis, set however within a very specific frame: The two media oversaw whether the Greek governments were efficient in implementing Troika's terms throughout the three Memoranda and their critique centred around any failure to do so, as this would jeopardise Greece's future. In that sense, the media studied legitimated their role as the watchdogs of the established order.

When it comes to the period around the third Memorandum, as both newspapers were not supportive of the Syriza government, their coverage was generally disapproving of its policy, even when the government fully implemented the bailout-related terms. As mentioned earlier, *I Kathimerini* has generally been sympathetic of a conservative, liberal management, while *Ta Nea* took a clear position against the Syriza government after it became part of Marinakis's media company. Within this vein, both newspapers frequently adopted Troika's discourse to delegitimate Syriza during the early phase of its government, in 2015, when the left party was resisting Troika's terms, by presenting Syriza as dangerous for Greece's future (Serafis and Herman 2018). Also, during the time around the "exodus" from the third Memorandum, in 2018, the government was presented as populist and dishonest, often downplaying or trivialising any (announced) measures targeted at easing economic pressure for certain social groups.

The study does not claim that its findings are representative of the situation in the entire media spectrum in Greece. Within mainstream print media in general, and even within the two newspapers studied, there has been a variety of opinions expressed, especially in editorials, which were not examined here, as the research focussed on "neutral" texts of event reporting. In opinion-oriented pieces, columnists would occasionally condemn Troika and the implemented policy, while there was often a personal or emotional tone focussing on the effects that the crisis and the implemented measures were having on people's lives (Kuntz 2016). Additionally, if pro-governmental media had been studied, the image may have been different. In a similar vein, since this study did not examine alternative media, which are generally reproachful of Memoranda-led neoliberal policies, potential alternative or more diverse representations of the crisis and the Memoranda, were not captured (see, e.g. Touri and Kostarella 2017).

Still, the news reports that were examined are representative of these two leading newspapers' stance and they also reflect persistent journalistic practices that extend beyond specific media. It should not be forgotten that *Ta Nea* and *I Kathimerini* are among the most prominent Greek newspapers and part of the leading media groups in the country. Furthermore, at the moment there are no alternative news media that are influential enough to communicate to a wide audience the counterhegemonic discourse they may be hosting. Additionally, after Syriza came into power, some of the country's left media (that have had some visibility) were supportive of its governmental policy, which made efforts to articulate a genuinely counter-hegemonic discourse more difficult (Mylonas 2018, 284–5).

One of the study's restrictions concerns the non-exhaustive contextualisation of the research findings in their social and political environment, due to length limitations, but more importantly, due to the impossibility of full contextualisation, no matter how extensive a piece of research is. There is always a disciplinary anchor, which in our case is media studies. In our research, the focus has been on news-as-discourse, comprising the produced news, the journalistic practices, and the broader socio-political environment that reflects and is reflected in the news. Within this logic, the broader environment was brought into the analysis in the instances and to the degree that it was necessary for the comprehension of what was examined each time, rendering, in these instances, contextualisation an organic component of the analysis. This practice is rather common in CDA and the cultural studies approaches that our research draws from.

Despite the limitations of this study, it can be argued that the main discourses identified and their mechanisms are in operation in both anti-Memorandum and pro-Memorandum legitimation efforts that have been employed in the news texts analysed, by the Greek government, the opposition, and international actors. Furthermore, our study's findings seem to reflect a rather consistent journalistic practice related to journalists' authority building that traverses political orientation. The CDA–cultural studies approach, in combination with the integration of the dual factual/narrative logic of news that our research adopted, allowed us to study discourse as practice by highlighting the cultural and ideological dimensions of this practice.

Regarding the media's broader role in the construction of the crisis reality, it has been argued that the mainstream media in Greece has been supporting the hegemonic discourse over the economic crisis and its handling, maintaining a pro-Memorandum stance (Doudaki et al. 2016; Doudaki 2015; Mylonas 2014; Arrese 2018). This stance is not necessarily or exclusively attributed to the media's affiliation with political parties, but it reflects its status as an institution that ideologically supports the established capitalist order. The print newspapers may not have the leading role they had in the past as privileged spaces for the articulation of society's (hegemonic and counter-hegemonic) discourses, but are still part of this space. Their cultural–symbolic capital is still relevant, extending their shrinking circulations.

The still-not-overcome economic crisis finds the political system in Greece in a state of high antagonism. The current era of polarisation in political life is reflected in the media's operation and its coverage of the crisis. The media in Greece struggle over resources in an impoverished (both in terms of economic resources and the position of journalists) environment (Siapera et al. 2015), where the culture of co-orientation of political forces and the media continues to exist, and is even reinforced, as it intertwines with the fierce struggle of political forces over power.

The economic crisis has left the Greek media scarred. The pauperisation of media organisations and the journalistic profession, in an environment of fierce attacks against ideological opponents that are articulated by and through the media, has had a significant impact on diversity and pluralism. The efforts for the elimination of (political) opponents and the ostracism of those who hold different opinions is becoming the norm in public life, witnessed broadly (e.g. among citizens on social media). Under these conditions, journalism in Greece does not seem to have the strength nor the societal support necessary to escape extreme polarisation and to remedy its weaknesses. Despite this bleak picture – not only for journalism but also for democratic practice – one should acknowledge that Greek journalists exhibit enhanced awareness regarding the pathogenies of the profession. In addition, there are several initiatives for the establishment of independent media and journalistic cooperative projects led by Greek journalists (Siapera et al. 2015), that engage in high-standard journalistic practices. The picture is complemented by a variety of alternative-activist media that are operative in the country, and which, albeit in most cases marginal, still articulate a counter-hegemonic discourse, regularly scrutinising both political and journalistic practices. Journalism has found in the past – at different times and in different situations (also in Greece) – a way to respond to challenges and revive itself, rising above its circumstances and leading the way in democratic struggles. The book ends with the wish that this time for Greek journalism will come soon.

Note

1 Regarding media's monitorial role, see, e.g. Christians et al. (2009).

References

Arrese, Ángel. 2018. "Austerity Policies in the European Press: A Divided Europe?" In *The Media and Austerity: Comparative Perspectives*, edited by Laura Basu, Steve Schifferes, and Sophie Knowles, 183–95. London: Routledge.

Christians, Clifford, Theodore Glasser, Denis McQuail, Kaarle Nordenstreng, and Robert White. 2009. *Normative Theories of the Media: Journalism in Democratic Societies*. Urbana, IL: University of Illinois Press.

Doudaki, Vaia. 2015. "Legitimation Mechanisms in the Bailout Discourse." *Javnost: The Public* 22 (1): 1–17.

Doudaki, Vaia, Angeliki Boubouka, Lia-Paschalia Spyridou, and Christos Tzalavras. 2016. "Dependency, (Non)Liability and Austerity News Frames of Bailout Greece." *European Journal of Communication* 31 (4): 426–45.

Goddard, Peter. 1998. "Press Rhetoric and Economic News: A Case Study." In *The Economy, Media and Public Knowledge*, edited by Neil T. Gavin, 71–89. London: Leicester University Press.

Kuntz, Maria Elena. 2016. "How the Greek Press Constructed the 'Greek Economic Crisis'." Master Thesis, Denver, CO: University of Denver.

Mylonas, Yiannis. 2014. "Crisis, Austerity and Opposition in Mainstream Media Discourses of Greece." *Critical Discourse Studies* 11 (3): 305–21.

Mylonas, Yiannis. 2018. "Hegemonic and Counter-Hegemonic Discourses of the Cypriot Economic Crisis by Greek Media." In *Cyprus and Its Conflicts: Representations, Materialities, and Cultures*, edited by Vaia Doudaki and Nico Carpentier, 268–89. New York: Berghahn Books.

Reshef, Yonatan, and Charles Keim. 2014. *Bad Time Stories: Government-Union Conflicts and the Rhetoric of Legitimation Strategies*. Toronto: University of Toronto Press.

Serafis, Dimitris, and Thierry Herman. 2018. "Media Discourse and Pathos: Sketching a Critical and Integrationist Approach: Greek and French Headlines before the Greek Referendum of 2015." *Social Semiotics* 28 (2): 184–200.

Siapera, Eugenia, Lambrini Papadopoulou, and Fragiskos Archontakis. 2015. "Post-Crisis Journalism." *Journalism Studies* 16 (3): 449–65.

Touri, Maria, and Ioanna Kostarella. 2017. "News Blogs Versus Mainstream Media: Measuring the Gap through a Frame Analysis of Greek Blogs." *Journalism* 18 (9): 1206–24.

Index

Note: Numbers in italics indicate figures, and numbers in bold indicate tables on the corresponding page.

For Product Safety Concerns and Information please contact our EU representative GPSR@taylorandfrancis.com
Taylor & Francis Verlag GmbH, Kaufingerstraße 24, 80331 München, Germany

www.ingramcontent.com/pod-product-compliance
Ingram Content Group UK Ltd.
Pitfield, Milton Keynes, MK11 3LW, UK
UKHW020939200926
475569UK00011B/17

* 9 7 8 0 3 6 7 1 8 3 9 4 3 *